Key Terms in Translation Studies

Also available from Continuum

Key Terms in Linguistics
Howard Jackson

Key Terms in Semiotics
Bronwen Martin and Felizitas Ringham

Key Terms in Syntax and Syntactic Theory
Silvia Luraghi and Claudia Parodi

Forthcoming titles:

Key Terms in Corpus Linguistics
Michaela Mahlberg and Matthew Brook O'Donnell

Key Terms in Pragmatics
Nicholas Allott

Key Terms in Second Language Acquisition
Alessandro G. Benati

Key Terms in Semantics
M. Lynne Murphy

Key Terms in Systemic Functional Linguistics
Christian Matthiessen, Kazuhiro Teruya and Marvin Lam

Key Terms in Translation Studies

Giuseppe Palumbo

continuum

Continuum International Publishing Group

The Tower Building   80 Maiden Lane
11 York Road   Suite 704
London SE1 7NX   New York NY 10038

British Library Cataloguing-in-Publication Data
A catalogue record for this book is available from the British Library.

ISBN: 978-0-8264-9824-3   (hardback)
        978-0-8264-9825-0   (paperback)

Library of Congress Cataloging-in-Publication Data
The Publisher has applied for CIP data

Typeset by Newgen Imaging Systems Pvt Ltd, Chennai, India
Printed and bound in Great Britain by Antony Rowe, Wiltshire.

Contents

Acknowledgements

Many friends and colleagues helped me in identifying the themes and ideas that went into this book. I am deeply indebted to: Federica Scarpa, Margaret Rogers, Maria Teresa Musacchio, Lawrence Venuti, David Katan, Chris Taylor and Dimitris Asimakoulas. Other friends have accepted to read and comment on early, partial drafts of the book. My sincere thanks go to Nadja Blondet, Silvia Cacchiani and Annalisa Sezzi. I am also particularly grateful to Marina Bondi, Marc Silver and other colleagues at the University of Modena and Reggio Emilia, who were enormously patient with me as I combined work on this book with my duties as a teacher and researcher there. Thanks, finally, to the Library staff at the School for Interpreters and Translators of the University of Trieste for their patience and assistance.

Abbreviations used

MT   machine translation
SL   source language
ST   source text
TL   target language
TT   target text

Introduction

Although translation has been practised and discussed for millennia, systematic interest in translation at a scholarly level has emerged quite recently and a distinct discipline having translation as its core object of research may be seen to have developed only over the last three decades. One of the founding statements of translation studies is conventionally identified with James H. Holmes' paper 'The Name and Nature of Translation Studies', delivered at a conference held in Copenhagen in 1972 but only available in printed form to a wide audience several years later. This was also the paper that provided a label for the field, previously referred to, in English, with various other labels including *translation theory* or *translatology*.

Starting from the 1940s and up to the 1970s, the study of translation was commonly seen as falling within the scope of applied linguistics, a view which was also related to the attempts carried out in those years at developing machine translation systems. The basic thrust of research on translation was therefore of an applied nature, even in most of the cases where reflection was presented as having a 'theoretical' nature. Results of research also found application in the training institutes that were being founded, especially in Europe, as a way of responding to the increasing demand for professional translators (a true explosion in the offer of training programmes for translators and interpreters would occur, at least in Europe, in the 1990s).

Early linguistic approaches looked at translation essentially from a contrastive point of view and mainly in terms of isolated stretches of language, especially at word or sentence level. Soon, however, interest in other levels of linguistic description emerged and, based on work carried out in text linguistics, discourse analysis and pragmatics, translation came to be looked at as a re-creation of texts.

In the meantime, the introduction of other disciplinary perspectives contributed to widen the scope of translation research: information theory and communication studies brought to translation an explicitly social dimension, emphasizing its nature as an action that involves other participants beside the translator (e.g. clients and readers) and is subject to considerations that go well beyond linguistic factors. In short, functional considerations at various levels were introduced in the study of translation and this represented a further move towards expanding the scope of translation research.

A strong interest in translation has traditionally been shown by literary studies and philosophy, which constitute another important source of ideas and themes that have been channelled into contemporary translation studies. Historically, discourse on translation has almost exclusively taken the form of commentaries on translation work carried out on literary and philosophical works or sacred texts (especially the Bible). Indeed, the oldest approach to translation can probably be seen to be the one based on hermeneutics, where translation is taken as a paradigm for wider problems of understanding and interpretation. Literary studies have contributed to research on translation ideas first elaborated in comparative literature and in cultural studies, ranging from notions such as that of 'system' or 'norm' to the issues linked to the representation of different cultural identities. Hermeneutic approaches, revived by poststructuralist and deconstructionist perspectives, have recently brought to the fore questions such as intertextuality and the uncontrollable polysemy of language, while at the same time continuing to investigate how translations can do justice to SL authors in spite of the incommensurability of languages – a concern felt as early as the first quarter of the 19th century, when the German theologian Friedrich Schleiermacher discussed whether translators should bring foreign authors to readers or whether they should lead readers to the foreign authors (his own preference was for the latter option).

James H. Holmes' programme of research as delineated in the 1972 paper mentioned above envisaged the creation of a descriptive branch in translation studies, i.e. one studying the phenomena of translating and translations without the largely prescriptive bias that Holmes detected in most existing research on the subject. A group of researchers coming from different backgrounds has, starting from the 1970s, worked for the development of such a branch, thus leading to one of the changes of paradigm that helped establish translation studies as an independent discipline. Descriptive approaches operated a complete reversal of perspective with respect to earlier research, focusing on translated texts as facts of the target culture and studying the socio-cultural and linguistic conditions in which these texts come about. A similar focus on constraints and influencing factors is to be found in another area that has recently received increased attention from the part of researchers, i.e. the study of the cognitive processes involved in the act of translation.

Holmes' proposal also entailed a clear separation between the two branches of 'pure research' (theory and description) and the applied branch of the discipline, i.e. the one concerned with translator training, the development of translation aids and the assessment of translations. While this position has for some time met with approval in a significant section of the field, such a sharp distinction is today being called into question, and an increasing number of scholars are working on aspects that straddle Holmes' the lines of internal disciplinary demarcation as proposed by Holmes.

Based on all of the above, the marked interdisciplinary nature of contemporary translation studies (drawing from linguistics, literary studies, philosophy, sociology, cultural studies, computer science and psychology, but the list is certainly incomplete) should have been made evident. For the purposes of the present work, aimed at presenting the key concepts of the discipline, such marked interdisciplinarity automatically rules out any attempt at exhaustiveness. The number of titles on translation published in the last few years and the proliferation of different perspectives and angles from which translation is being observed and researched is such that encompassing all relevant concepts and taking stock of innovative notions all in one work is an unattainable ideal. The list of key terms and concepts presented here is therefore to be regarded as necessarily selective, and certainly also influenced by the particular perspective adopted by the author in his own research on translation. An attempt has been made, however, at ensuring that most current perspectives on translation are represented, and that at least some of their central concepts are included. At any rate, the terms and concepts presented in the book have been chosen so as to represent no more than an *introductory* survey of the discipline. The section called 'Key Thinkers in Translation Studies' presents brief sketches of the work carried out by scholars whose ideas have proved particularly influential in the recent development of the discipline. Even more than for the selection of key concepts, the inclusion of these particular scholars and not others is ultimately to be seen as a personal, subjective decision. In general, another decisive source of bias in the selection has certainly been the preference accorded to theories and research reported on in English. Finally, a decision has been taken to restrict the present survey to current research on translation and thus leave out interpreting – today probably a separate field in its own right and, as such, deserving of wider, and more competent, treatment.

Key Terms in Translation Studies

Abusive fidelity

Philip E. Lewis (1985: 43) calls 'abusive fidelity' a mode of translation that 'values experimentation, tampers with usage, seeks to match the polyvalencies and plurivocities or expressive stresses of the original by producing its own'. Such a practice is seen as particularly suitable for texts that involve substantial conceptual density or complex literary effects, e.g. poetry and philosophy. Venuti (2003: 252–257) sees this kind of translating as abusive in two senses: it resists the structures and discourses of the target language and culture, and especially the pressure towards idiomatic usage and transparent style; in so doing, it also interrogates the structures and discourses of the source text, uncovering its potentialities of meaning.

Acceptability

In the theory of translation **norms** as elaborated by G. Toury (1980, 1995), 'acceptability' is the result of the translator's initial decision to subject him-/herself to the norms prevailing in the target culture. A translation is thus 'acceptable' in the sense that it subscribes to the 'the linguistic and literary norms active in the TL and in the target literary polysystem or a certain section of it' (Toury 1980: 54). Subscription to the norms prevailing in the SL would, on the other hand, lead to an 'adequate' translation (see also Toury 1995: 56–58).

In a more general sense, but mainly in relation to assessment carried out in the context of **specialist translation**, acceptability refers to the adherence of the TT to the norms and conventions of text production prevailing in the TL (Vermeer 1996: 78; see also Scarpa 2008: 207–213). This implies taking into consideration aspects that may vary according to the particular purpose served by the translation and the expectations of readers. From a linguistic-textual point of view, the conventions to be taken into account may go from aspects of textual organization or register to details of spelling and punctuation.

See also: **adequacy, accuracy, assessment, quality**.

Accuracy

In a general sense, the notion of accuracy is often referred to in discussing the correctness of a given translation; in this general sense, then, an 'accurate' translation (of a word, an utterance or an entire text) is equivalent to a 'good' or 'right' translation, with no further specifications. In discussing the **assessment** of translations, however, the term is sometimes used in a narrower sense and distinguished from other parameters of assessment. In the context of **specialist translation**, for instance, accuracy normally refers to the extent to which a TT reflects the ST in terms of content. Other assessment parameters include **adequacy** and **acceptability** and take into account such aspects as the suitability of the TT to its communicative purpose or its adherence to TL norms of text production.

See also: **quality**.

Adaptation

The term tends to be applied to forms of translation where a considerable distance from the formal and lexical aspects of the ST can be observed. For short segments or parts of a text, adaptation can be seen as a **translation technique** addressing specific differences between the SL and the TL in terms of situational contexts and cultural references. An ST segment may thus need to be adapted in translation when it has no lexical equivalents in the TL, when the situation it refers is not familiar to TL readers or when a close translation would be inappropriate in functional terms. These criteria are of course bound to be considered in relative terms, as they ultimately depend on a consideration of the TL readers' needs or expectations. Vinay and Darbelnet ([1958] 1995: 39) include adaptation in their seven translation procedures. Their own example is a translation of the English *He kissed his daughter on the mouth* with the French *Il serra tendrement sa fille dans ses bras* ('He tenderly hugged his daughter'), felt to be more appropriate than the literal *Il embrassa sa fille sur la bouche.*

At a global level, adaptation may be seen as a general **translation strategy** or mode of text transfer aimed at reconstructing the purpose, function or impact of the general text (Bastin 1998). It may be opted for by the translator him-/herself or required by external factors (i.e. editorial policy). Procedures of adaptation in this sense include expansion, omission and the re-creation of whole ST sections aimed at preserving the general function of the text. Adaptation in this sense tends to be associated with particular contexts or genres such as **theatre translation**, **audiovisual translation**, advertising and children's literature. These are characterized by a high degree of interplay between linguistic text and other aspects such as image and sound. A recurring debate concerns the point at which adaptation ceases to be translation and becomes a 'freer' re-creation of the ST. As, historically, the concept of translation has been observed to show enormous variability, scholars are today inclined to include adaptation within translation, as long as the text presented as an adaptation is based on a source text.

It is interesting to note that to people who are not directly involved in professional translation or come to translation via different routes from academic study or training, adaptation always seems to suggest something different from 'mere' translation, the latter being identified essentially with an interlinear, literal version of the ST. Illuminating accounts in this respect are provided in Snell-Hornby (2006: 87–90) with reference to theatre translation and film **dubbing**, contexts where translators are sometimes seen to play secondary roles as providers of a text which is then passed on to someone else for a 'creative' rewriting.

Adequacy

The notion of adequacy has often been used in the literature on translation to characterize the relationship between the ST and the TT, with different scholars attaching more or less different senses to the term. In the theory of translation **norms** as elaborated by G. Toury (1980, 1995), 'adequacy' is the result of the translator's initial decision to subject him-/herself to the norms prevailing in the source culture. A translator thus produces an adequate translation when (provided the basic rules of the TL system are not breached), he or she subscribes to 'the original text, with its textual relations and the norms expressed by it and contained by it' (Toury 1980: 54). Subscriptions to the norms active in the TL, on the other hand, would lead to an 'acceptable' translation. Adequacy and acceptability are the two extremes implied by the 'initial norm' that, from a theoretical point of view, Toury (1995: 56–58) sees as guiding the translator's decisions at both micro- and macro-contextual level. Actual translation decision often imply 'some ad hoc combination of, or compromise' (Toury 1995: 57) between these two extremes.

In relation to the **assessment** of translations, especially when carried out in the context of **specialist translation**, the term adequacy may refer to the extent to which a translated text conforms to the **translation brief**, from the point of view of both the communicative purpose of the text and the procedural aspects of the translation task (Scarpa 2008: 211–213). A translated text is thus considered 'adequate' when, in the TL, it serves the purpose it is meant to serve according to the brief and when it has been produced following the procedure established by the brief or otherwise agreed between the client and the translator. In short, adequacy is generally taken to refer to aspects related to the process of translation and particularly to the balance between the time and money spent on the task and the quality of the text.

See also: **acceptability, accuracy, quality**.

Agency

The sociological notion of agency has to do with the capacity of individual subjects to act purposefully in a social context. It has recently attracted the attention of translation scholars interested in looking at the interplay between translators as individual subjects and the contexts in which they operate, the latter being described in terms of social and ideological values or as networks of power relations (see e.g. Gouanvic 1997; Pym 1998; Wolf 2002). The notion has come to the fore both in studies of translation adopting a sociological perspective and in **poststructuralist** and **cultural studies approaches**, i.e. those that pay particular attention to the complex of social factors and individual intentionalities forming the scenario in which translation takes place. In particular, one question that scholars have started to investigate is the *degree* of agency, i.e. of choice, of individual translators – a question that may be seen to have links to issues of **power** and **ideology**, to the concept of *habitus*, but also to questions such as the level of **creativity** implied by translation. Agency may thus be seen to refer to how translators act at the interface between individual and social dimensions.

Discussions of agency can often be seen to take an 'activist' stance as they conform to research programmes aimed at reconsidering the role and visibility of translators. Agency is also sometimes taken as a point of departure for attempting a shift of perspective in the way translation and translators are conceptualized. Scholars such as Tymoczko (2005) are re-examining translation as a practice, characterizing it as a group process (as in some non-Western theories) rather than the result of an individual endeavour. This view also rests on a consideration of the changing scenarios in modern-day **professional translation** practice, in particular the new working conditions of translators as brought about by the process of **globalization** and the introduction of new technologies, especially computer networks. Translation is more than ever a collective endeavour as translators become part of teams operating in online environments. Translation jobs are, as a consequence, configured as 'team projects' going through successive stages of 'production'. This is seen as a significant factor in descriptions of agency, as translation becomes an increasingly decentred process and translation choices are less easily traced back to individual decisions.

Assessment

Assessment (or evaluation) is the activity aimed at establishing the **quality** of a translated text. As the notion of quality is a relative one, assessment is also bound to rely on relative criteria, depending on the aims of assessment and the context in which a translated text is assessed. Chesterman (1997: Chap. 5) proposes a broad distinction between 'descriptive assessment' and 'evaluative assessment'. The former is aimed at determining the nature or the characteristics of a translation (i.e. what a translation is like), the aim being that of inferring the translator's concept of equivalence (as in Toury 1995: 36–39) or of describing the social and cultural conditions under which translations are produced (which is the focus of interest for the scholars looking at translation from a cultural studies perspective). Evaluative assessment, on the other hand, is made 'in terms of how good or bad a translation is' (Chesterman 1997: 119).

With regard to evaluative assessment, a distinction can be made between assessment carried out in a professional context and assessment that takes place in contexts of translator training (cf. Scarpa 2008: 207–212). In professional translation, the criteria guiding assessment may have to do as much with the translated text as with the process that led to them. This type of assessment will thus take into consideration (and variously prioritize) aspects having to do with the adherence of the TT to the **translation brief** (in terms of the communicative purpose of the TT or the specifications provided for the job), the procedure adopted to arrive at the TT, and, crucially, the time taken by the translator to complete the job. Assessment in a translator training context (often called 'formative assessment') generally has different aims (Chesterman 1997: 138–141). It can be directed at giving feedback to trainees so that they can improve their future translations or it can be aimed at accreditation, i.e. a certification that a translator has reached a given level of **competence**.

Compared to assessment carried out in professional, real-life situations, formative assessment tends to be based on 'ideal' criteria, but the two need not be seen as opposites (cf. Scarpa 2008: 207–208) – formative assessment may well take into consideration criteria typical of real-life scenarios, whereas assessment at professional level may often include a consideration of linguistic and textual features, not only where **acceptability** for the TL public is concerned but also in terms of **accuracy** in rendering ST terminology or in transmitting specialist content. A central concept in all forms of assessment is that of **translation error**, although the types and gravity scales considered for translation errors will vary according to the specific aim of the assessment. For example, in professional settings there may be cases where a spelling mistake or a text formatting error are considered more serious errors than questionable TL lexical choices (which, by contrast, may be one of the cornerstones of formative assessment).

From a more explicitly scholarly viewpoint, assessment has traditionally taken place in the domain of literary translation and mostly with reference to the product of translation, i.e. texts. Scholars have tried to lay down the principles whereby translated texts should be assessed in relation to the original and to an assumed 'ideal' translation. More recently, however, this notion of an ideal translation has been problematized, while the work of some scholars (e.g. Venuti 1995, 1998) has been directed at changing the public's perception of what a good translation is or should be, thereby trying to influence the quality assumptions on the part of publishers, TT readers and translators themselves. Other recent works on assessment proposed at academic level embrace a wider range of text types. A model explicitly aimed at translation quality assessment from an evaluative point of view, and one to be applied to a wide range of text types, is House's (1977, 1997), which is based on analysis of the ST-TT relation centred around a Hallidayan, systemic-functional view of register. Target-oriented theories of translation such as **skopos** **theory** have also been seen as providing useful parameters for assessment, essentially giving prominence to the purpose served by the translated text (see Nord 1991, 1997).

Audio description

The term refers to a form of voiced narration used to make films, TV programmes and theatre performances available to blind and visually impaired people. It provides a recorded account of what happens on the screen or on stage, describing the action, the body language of characters and the scenery. The description is provided in between dialogues and must not interfere with important sound-effects. The information thus provided should not overburden the listeners but at the same time it should supply all necessary detail.

Audiovisual translation

The term audiovisual translation refers to the translation of texts contained in audiovisual products, i.e. products combining sound and video components, such as films and TV programmes (Gambier and Gottlieb 2001; Gambier 2004; Orero 2004). These products are often described as 'multimodal' texts, that is, texts relying on a wide range of semiotic resources or 'modes': not only spoken text but also gesture, gaze, movement, sound, colours, written language and so on. The meaning of a multimodal text (e.g. a film or a TV ad) is seen as the composite product of the different selected semiotic resources (which is true, in fact, for most type of written texts, but usually to a lesser degree). As a way of emphasizing such 'multimodality', the term audiovisual translation has been gradually gaining ground over competing labels such as *film* or *screen translation* (both of which are still widely used; *multimedia translation* is another label sometimes used for this area of practice and research). Forms of audiovisual translation include the long-established practices of **subtitling** and **dubbing** as well as more recent forms such as **voice-over** and **audio description**.

Subtitling and dubbing remain the two major forms of audiovisual translation. Dubbing, which is the more expensive of the two, has traditionally been the preferred option in countries with large markets and a homogeneous linguistic community (e.g. Germany or Italy). Subtitling tends to be preferred in smaller markets or in countries where dubbing is not felt to be an affordable investment. In the last few years, however, as the market of audiovisual products sees an increasing diversification in both the types of products and the channels of distribution, the division is less clear-cut and in bigger countries the more common forms of audiovisual transfer are combined with other, previously uncommon types.

Research on audiovisual translation has so far looked at how translators' decision-making is affected by the particular medium of the translation (e.g. subtitling as against dubbing), how translators cope with the problem of synchronizing TL text to SL speech and to images, and how the social, cultural and geographical differences emerging in SL texts (e.g. in films) are handled in translation.

Back-translation

A back-translation is a word-for-word translation of a target text, or a stretch of it, back into the source language. This is normally intended to illustrate either the target text or the translation process to an audience that does not understand the target language.

Binary error, see **error**.

'Black-box' analogy

In relation to the cognitive and psycholinguistic processes involved in translation, the mind of the translator is often characterized as 'black-box', so as to remark the fact that those kinds of processes are available for study only indirectly. In other words, researchers cannot 'peer into the black-box' of translators – they can only make inferences on what goes on in their minds through empirical studies such as those carried out in **process-oriented research**.

Borrowing

The term refers to the carrying over of a word or expression from the ST to the TT, either to fill a lexical gap in the TL or to achieve a particular stylistic effect. A word such as *lasagne* in Italian may be borrowed because it has no equivalents, while *siesta* in Spanish may be translated as *rest* or *nap*, or borrowed for stylistic effect. Some borrowings become so well-established in a language that they are no longer regarded as such. The decision whether to translate a given SL word with a borrowing ultimately depends on such factors as the purpose of the translation and the type of TL audience.

Calque

The term refers to a **translation technique** applied to an SL expression and involving the literal translation of its component elements. Vinay and Darbelnet ([1958] 1995) distinguish between lexical calques, which respect the TL syntactic structure, and structural calques, which introduce a new syntactic structure in the TL. With reference to English and French, an example of lexical calque is the translation of *Compliments of the Season* with *Compliments de la saison*, while translating *science fiction* with *science-fiction* is a structural calque.

Cannibalism

In literary translation, an approach proposed by the Brazilian poets and translators Augusto and Haroldo de Campos in which the translator is equated with a cannibal consuming the flesh of writers and benefiting from their strength (see Vieira 1999). As cannibals, translators take, and do with their ST, what they please, their purpose being that of benefiting the target culture. STs thus become food to be digested and exploited for purposes that are different from those of the original texts.

Category shift

For Catford (1965), a type of translation **shift** that involves changing the category of the SL item (with categories described following Hallidayan grammar). In particular, the four categories considered by Catford (1965: 73f.) in describing shifts are: unit, structure, class and system. The category of *unit* includes the following elements: sentences, clauses, group, words and morphemes, which are seen to form a scale of 'ranks'. Translating a word with a phrase would be an example of a unit shift, as in the translation of *Be prepared to* . . . with *Preparati a* . . . in Italian, where the English verbal group comprising a predicative adjective corresponds to a single verb in Italian (a literal translation would have been: 'Sii preparato a . . .').

Structure refers to the internal organization of units, e.g. into subject, predicator and complement if considered at clause rank, or into modifier and head if seen at group rank. An example provided by Catford for a shift at clause rank is the translation of the English sentence *John loves Mary* into Gaelic: *Tha gradh aig Iain air Mairi* (back-translated as 'Is love at John on Mary').

Class is a particular grouping or set that a given unit belongs to (e.g. nouns vs verbs or modifiers vs qualifiers). Translating the English *a medical student* into *un étudiant en médecine* in French involves a category shift in terms of the change from *medical* (a modifier) into *en médecine* (a qualifier) as well as the change from adjective (*medical*) into noun (*médecine*).

Finally, in relation to the category of *system* Catford identifies *intra-system shifts*, i.e. cases where the shifts occur within a closed set of alternatives, such as active/passive or singular/plural, between languages where these sets of alternatives largely correspond. The translation of *advice* (singular) with *des conseils* (plural) in French represents an intra-system shift as normally English singular nouns are translated with French singular nouns.

See also: **level shift, rank-bound translation, unbounded translation**.

Coherence

The related notions of coherence and **cohesion** concern the way utterances or texts are organized so as to constitute meaningful and integrated wholes. In particular, coherence refers to the ways in which an utterance is seen to establish meaningful relations between its parts from a conceptual (i.e. semantic or logical) point of view (cohesion, on the other hand, has to do with the connections established in the surface text by lexical and grammatical devices). Coherence depends on the organization of the utterance as much as on the receiver's interpretation of it, which in turn changes according to the receiver's expectations and knowledge of the world. Thus, a single sentence such as 'Have you bought it yet?' constitutes a coherent whole only inasmuch as the hearer can, according to the **context** or situation, easily interpret the reference for 'it' (a DVD, a book, a house, etc.). In longer texts, coherence results from the relations established between sentences, which speaker or writers may organize according to different types of sequences (e.g. narrative, causal or argumentative). Again, however, the interpretation of such relations and sequences implies an active role on the part of readers, whose knowledge and presuppositions play a crucial role in establishing relations between different parts of a text. In translation, such knowledge and presuppositions may not be the same for ST and TT readers. This may affect the translator's decision as regards a variety of aspects, ranging from intersentential links (which may have to be made more explicit) to the treatment of elements as diverse as pronouns, metaphors and **culture-bound terms** which, if not transparent enough for the TT reader, may affect the way he or she makes sense of the text (for coherence and explicitation, see Blum Kulka 1986). In short, the notion of coherence has much to do with aspects of pragmatic equivalence in translation (see Baker 1992: Chap. 7).

Cohesion

The related notions of cohesion and **coherence** concern the way utterances or texts are organized so as to constitute meaningful and integrated wholes. In particular, cohesion refers to the ways in which an utterance establishes meaningful relations between its elements by using grammatical and lexical devices. An utterance is said to be *cohesive* when its elements can be interpreted with reference to other elements within the **co-text**. Cohesion thus establishes relations at the surface level of language, whereas coherence concerns conceptual relations underlying the surface text.

Following the model of cohesion elaborated by Halliday and Hasan (1976), two broad classes of cohesive devices can be identified: grammatical and lexical devices. Grammatical cohesive devices include *anaphora* (reference backwards in the text), *cataphora* (reference forwards in the text), *substitution* and *ellipsis* (i.e. reference to other elements in the text by replacement or by omission of certain elements respectively), and conjunctions. In the following exchange taken from a hypothetical ongoing conversation:

A: *Have they moved?*
B: *No, but they will soon – to the more expensive one*

'they' is an anaphoric reference to people mentioned earlier in the conversation, 'will' is the auxiliary for the omitted main verb (a case of contrastive ellipsis), 'but' is a conjunction and 'one' is a case of substitution for a referent (a house or flat) that was mentioned earlier. In this other sentence:

As a boy, he would never watch football. Later, John became one of Aresenal's wildest supporters

the noun group 'a boy' and the pronoun 'he' are both cataphoric references to 'John'. Lexical cohesion is primarily established through *reiteration* and *collocation*. Reiteration comprises the repetition of lexical items (repetition of the exact form of a word or of morphologically distinct forms) or the use of items that are semantically related (through relations such as synoymy, hyponymy, meronymy and antonymy). **Collocation** is the tendency of words to occur in regular combinations and can be seen as a cohesive device in that it contributes to textuality and generates expectations in hearers/readers. Thus, in a text about journalism, mentions of *freedom* (and not *liberty*) *of the press* are very likely in English. As far as translation is concerned, the relevance of cohesion lies in the fact that different languages prefer certain sets of cohesive devices over others (see Baker 1992: Chap. 6).

Colligation

The term refers to a particular form of **collocation** involving relationships at the grammatical rather than at the lexical level. In other words, a colligation is either the frequent co-occurrence between a given word or phrase and words belonging to a certain grammatical class or the association of a word or phrase with a particular grammatical function. For example, as shown by the linguist Michael Hoey in his book *Lexical Priming* (2005), in English the phrase *in consequence* colligates with (i.e. is frequently found in) theme position (see **theme/rheme**) and has an aversion to being postmodified.

Collocation

The term collocation refers to the tendency of certain sets of words to occur regularly together, in such a way that the meaning of an individual word can be identified in relation to the words it 'collocates with'. The notion was first explicitly introduced by the British linguist J. R. Firth in the 1950s; it was then refined by M. A. K. Halliday and the late John M. Sinclair and became a central concept in their study of lexis and the way lexis interacts with syntax in the construction of units of meaning. In particular, Sinclair, and other researchers working in what became known as the Natural Language Processing community, exploited the increasing memory capacity of computers to store ever larger collections of authentic texts. In these, they tried to establish regular patterns of co-occurrence between given lexical items: the point was to show how the meaning of the individual items in such patterns can be described in relation to the patterns themselves, i.e. as a function of the linguistic (and ultimately situational) context in which an individual item appears. So, for instance, a noun such as *discussion* can be seen, in English, to be accompanied by a restricted set of adjectives (as in *a heated discussion*), making it unlikely to find it combined with other adjectives having similar meaning (cf. *an inflamed discussion*). Attempts at describing the patterns entered into by lexical and grammatical items (see also **colligation**) are leading to a reconsideration of meaning, now seen by some linguists as constructed around units that may be larger than was previously assumed. Ultimately, this reconsideration may lead to questioning the way the interaction between grammar and lexis has traditionally been presented.

As far as translation is concerned, collocational appropriateness is one of the factors that are taken into account either at the moment of providing an appropriate TL equivalent or when evaluating a translated text. To go back to the example given above (*a heated discussion*), what should the equivalent for *heated* be in other languages? Taken alone, the word may have a set of possible equivalents in each of the languages considered, but it is highly probable that, when combined with the equivalent for *discussion*, only one or two of these equivalents will be preferred (cf. *une violente discussion* in French, *una discussione accesa* or *violenta* in Italian, and *una discusión acalorada* in Spanish).

Deviations from collocational patterns in the TL may in some cases give rise to criticisms (e.g. where translation aims at **acceptability** in the TL). In other cases, e.g. in fiction, advertisements or humour, unlikely collocations may be a motivated feature of the ST itself, which may have to be taken into account in providing TL equivalents. Baker (1992: 51) gives two examples of collocations showing an increased degree of 'markedness', or deviation from common collocational usage: one is *heavy gambler*, as opposed to the more usual *compulsive gambler*; the other, taken from a novel by John Le Carré, is in the sentence 'Could real peace break out?', where *peace* is seen to combine with *break out*, a verb normally associated with *war* (*peace* would normally *prevail*). Specialized domains have their own typical collocations which may not be reflected in general language usage. In economics, for instance, *growth* can be accompanied by adjectives such as *healthy*, *sustained* or *sluggish*; in translation, equivalent collocations may have to be used, especially when the TT is addressed to an audience of domain specialists.

Communicative translation

For Newmark (1981: 22, 39), this is a mode of translation that gives priority to the informative function of the ST or reproduces on TL readers the effect obtained on readers of the original. A communicative translation of the French *Défense de marcher sur le gazon* would be *Keep of the grass*, while a **semantic translation** would yield *Walking on the turf is forbidden* (Newmark 1981: 54). Communicative translation is presented by Newmark as suited for all those texts (the majority) where originality of expression is not an important aspect (see also **Peter Newmark** in the 'Key Thinkers' section).

Comparable corpus

In translation studies, the term is commonly used to refer to a collection of non-translated and translated texts selected according to principled criteria as regards proportion, textual genre, subject-matter domain and sampling period. In a broader sense, a comparable corpus is any collection of texts containing components in different languages 'that are collected using the same sampling frame and similar balance and representativeness' (McEnery and Xiao 2007: 20).

See also: **corpora, parallel corpus**.

Compensation

This term indicates the use of a **translation technique** aimed at making up for the loss of an ST effect, such as a pun or an alliteration. Two main types of compensation can be distinguished (cf. Harvey 1995): *compensation in kind* tries to re-create the ST effect by strategically using TL linguistic devices (e.g. turning an ST alliteration into a rhyme in the TL); *compensation in place* re-produces the effect in a different part of the text.

Competence

Translation competence has to do with what enables an individual to translate (a text, a sentence or an individual item) from one language to another. Traditionally, this competence tended to be equated with linguistic competence and no distinction was made between the competence of professional translators and that of bilingual individuals with no specific training in translation (or, at any rate, bilinguals not acting as professional translators). In recent years, the focus of interest is on translation competence as observed in professional translators. The specific areas of interest for researchers include: the particular strategies adopted by translators in performing a task; their competence in using **translation aids** and researching vocabulary; the way they develop and apply so-called 'translation routines', i.e. standard transfer operations leading to TL equivalents that are appropriate to the task at hand.

Translation competence is thus today understood as the set of knowledge, skills and attitudes that enable an individual to act as a professional translator, although there are scholars (e.g. Kiraly 2000) who still keep 'translation competence' distinct from 'translator competence'. Various studies (cf. Schäffner and Adab 2000; PACTE 2005) have investigated how translation competence develops or how it can be acquired by trainees. Little consensus remains, however, on how competence (whether it is *translator* or *translation* competence) can be defined in more detail, or what its distinctive components are. Following Pym (2003), in the various models of competence proposed so far, four tendencies can be identified: (1) competence as a summation of linguistic competencies (SL competence + TL competence), which is the more traditional view; (2) competence as 'no competence': as translation deals with the actual use of languages, Pym (2003: 484) notes that it would be paradoxical, in Chomskyan terms, to describe as 'competence' something which is really 'performance' – the term has thus variously been replaced by the scholars who took this approach with cognate notions such as 'proficiency', 'strategies', 'expertise', etc.; (3) competence as a multicomponential notion, i.e. one made up of several skills (but, as Pym notes, lists of skills can be expanded *ad infinitum*, thus proving scarcely useful from both a theoretical and applicative point of view); (4) competence as 'supercompetence', i.e. something which defines translating and nothing but translating. Pym (2003: 489) himself opts for a 'minimalist' notion of competence, seen as 'the ability to generate a series of more than one viable target text (TT_1, TT_2 . . . TT_n) for a pertinent source text (ST)' plus 'the ability to select only one viable TT from this series, quickly and with justified confidence'.

Componential analysis

The term refers to the analysis of the basic components of the meaning of a given word. It implies a view of lexical meaning as based on sense and sense components. For example, the word *bachelor* could be seen as having the following components: 'man', 'adult', 'unmarried'. As a method for analysing word meaning with a view to translation it is extensively treated in Nida (1964) and Newmark (1981). Once an SL word or expression is submitted to componential analysis, a TL equivalent can be chosen that matches the sense components relevant in the context at hand. So, for instance, the word *portière* in French may be seen to equate in English to 'door + of railway carriage or car', therefore *car door* or *carriage door* depending on the context. In particular, in a word or lexical unit a distinction can be made between referential and pragmatic sense components, the latter referring to aspects such as cultural context, connotation, degree of formality and even suggestive sound composition (as in onomatopoeia). Thus, *chair* in English and *Stuhl* in German could be seen to have the same referential sense components, while 'jolly' as in *jolly good* would have sense components associated with social class that the German intensifier *ganz* ('quite', as in *ganz gut*) does not share (Newmark 1988: 114–115).

Computer-assisted translation

Also called 'computer-aided translation', computer-assisted translation, or CAT, is translation carried out, generally at a professional level, with the help of specific computer tools aimed at improving the efficiency of the translation process. CAT was traditionally distinguished from fully automatic **machine translation** (MT), i.e. MT with no human intervention, and was seen to include human-aided MT and machine-aided human translation (Hutchins and Somers 1992). More recent typologies (e.g. in Quah 2006) revise this distinction and equate CAT with translation performed principally by humans using computerized tools (or, in other words, with machine-aided human translation). It is unanimously acknowledged, however, that clear-cut distinctions between these categories are becoming impossible as numerous tools integrate technologies that were once seen as belonging to one or the other category. MT, for instance, is sometimes used in combination with **translation memories**, a tool that is usually associated with CAT scenarios. Other tools associated with CAT are terminology management systems (see **termbase**) and the more specific software tools used in **localization**.

Connotative meaning

The connotative meaning of a linguistic expression is the emotive, affect-ive, largely context-independent component of meaning, distinguished from its more stable, **denotative meaning**. The word 'sunset' refers, denotatively, to the 'daily disappearance of the sun behind the horizon', while connotatively it might be associated either with romance or with the final stage in a period of time, e.g. in a person's life.

Context

This is a broad notion that can be used to refer to various aspects of the situation in which an act of translation takes place. According to the perspective adopted in observing a text, the context may refer either to the immediate situation or to the culture in which a text is produced or received. Historically, the importance of the notion of con-text was made evident by the work of Bronislaw Malinowski, a social anthropologist studying the Trobriand islanders of New Guinea in the second decade of the twentieth century. In carrying out his ethno-graphic work, Malinowski realized that, in order to provide English equivalents for the native language terms and texts that he wished to study, contextual specifications were often needed, i.e. reference had to be made to the situation and culture in which the linguistic items had originally been placed. Based on the work by Malinowski and, later, other linguists working within the same tradition (e.g. M. A. K. Halliday), a distinction is often made between the 'context of situ-ation', i.e. the immediate context in which an utterance is produced, and the 'context of culture', i.e. the institutions and customs of a given linguistic community. The term **co-text** is sometimes used to refer to the immediate linguistic context surrounding a given word or phrase.

Contrastive analysis

The term contrastive analysis refers to the study of a pair of languages aimed at observing differences and similarities between them at the phonological, syntactic and semantic levels. It is a kind of analysis frequent in studies of foreign language learning, where its aim is mostly that of observing cases of actual or potential interference between languages. Some foreign speakers of English, for example, may say *I don't see them for three years* (instead of *I haven't seen them . . .*) as a result of the negative influence exerted by the present tense used in similar sentences in their native language. Contrastive studies have traditionally compared languages at the systemic level, i.e. with little attention to the specific communicative contexts in which utterances take place, but in recent years they have also increasingly taken into account pragmatic aspects. Although contrastive linguists tend to draw a sharp demarcation line between contrastive analysis and the study of translation, it has been shown (cf. Chesterman 1998: 37f.) that the borderline between the two is a fuzzy one, as contrastive analysis is bound to resort to ideas of translation **equivalence** in the testing of its hypotheses, at least at the syntactic and semantic levels. As argued by Chesterman (1998: 39), both contrastive analysis and translation theory can be seen to be interested in how 'the same thing' can be said in two languages, although each field puts this information to different ends. Contrastive analysis, in particular, may be seen to aim at establishing the conditions under which two utterances may be seen to be potentially equivalent, while translation theory ultimately aims at explaining why translators opt for certain TL choices rather than others.

Conventionalization, see **normalization**.
Cooperative Principle, see **implicature**.

Corpora

Language corpora are collections of texts put together in a principled way and prepared for computer processing. They are being applied to an increasing number of studies in descriptive/empirical and applied linguistics. The first corpus-based studies of language appeared in the 1960s, but the significant growth in what came to be known as *corpus linguistics* occurred during the 1980s and 1990s, when scholars such as John M. Sinclair started to exploit the increasing memory capacity of computers to collect ever larger collection of authentic texts. Today corpora of texts in machine-readable form are available in a large number of languages. They are being used for purposes of research and as an aid to lexicographers engaged in dictionary making.

Corpora can be of different types. *General* corpora contain text of different types and not related to any specific domain. *Specialized* corpora contain texts of a particular type or relating to a particular domain. *Learner* corpora contain texts produced by learners of a second language. *Monitor* corpora are designed so as to track changes in language over time, while *historical* corpora contain texts from different historical periods. All of these types of corpora can be designed so as to include texts in more than one language. Besides translation-related research and practice (see below), multilingual corpora can be used to look at language-specific, typological and cultural differences, and for practical applications (mainly in language teaching and lexicography).

Signs of interest in corpus-based studies of translation emerged in the 1980s, when corpora were first used to describe the features characterizing translated texts (as opposed to non-translated texts). In particular, corpora were seen as lending themselves to the study of translation (especially literary translation, in the early stages) as advocated in G. Toury's descriptive approach. Within this approach, corpora could contribute to the identification of the **norms** implicitly adhered to by a community of translators.

It was in the 1990s, however, that the potential for corpus use in the study of translation became more apparent and a carefully defined programme of research was laid out (see Baker 1995, 1996; Laviosa 2002; Olohan 2004). Researchers have since been compiling different types of multilingual corpora (see **parallel corpus** and **comparable corpus**; notice that the terminology surrounding multilingual corpora is still somewhat confused). Various hypotheses about translation are being tested in such corpora, most of them coming under the 'umbrella' term **universals of translation** (a notion that itself evolved from the description of the above-mentioned translation norms; see also **product-oriented research**).

As far as translation practice is concerned, corpora are used as reference materials in translator training and are exploited in the development of **computer-assisted translation** systems and **machine translation** systems. In particular, they can serve as repositories of past translations (see **translation memory**), thus complementing dictionaries, or as archives of texts written in the language the translator works into (what were previously often called 'parallel' texts). These corpora can be used to check authentic usage in various scenarios: when translating into the second language; when translating texts from a specialized domain of which the translator is not an expert; when the translator fears interference from the source language. It is easy to imagine, however, that in such scenarios the internet has today become the first port of call for most professional translators.

Co-text

The term is often used to indicate the linguistic elements surrounding a given word or phrase, as distinguished from the situational, extra-linguistic **context** in which an utterance takes place.

Covert error

A type of error characterized in relation to the strategy of **covert translation** as identified by House (1977, 1997). Covert errors are mismatches between the ST and the TT along a functional dimension, i.e. TT elements that fail to establish functional equivalence with the corresponding ST elements. The identification of covert errors presupposes that the ST and the TT generate comparable expectations in the respective groups of readers, that no secondary function is added to the TT and that there is basic inter-translatability between the languages involved (i.e. that linguistic means are available to provide equivalents for such SL distinctions as that between *Du* and *Sie* in German as forms of address). Translation errors identified on the basis of an implicit comparison with comparable texts written by native speakers could also be seen as falling within this category. Such errors would have to do with aspects such as over- or under-use of a given word or structure or with unusual sentence length.

See also: **error, overt error**.

Covert translation

This is a term introduced by House (1977, 1997) to indicate a translation strategy leading to the creation of a text that 'enjoys the status of an original source text in the target culture' (1997: 69). In particular, a covert translation is one that reproduces the function of the ST where this function has no particular ties to the source culture. Texts that lead to a covert translation include scientific and economic texts, tourist brochures, journalistic texts and in general all 'authorless texts or texts that have dispensable authors' (House 1997: 163). The original and its covert translation need not, for House, be equivalent at the linguistic, textual and register level. At these levels the translator may legitimately manipulate the original using what House calls a 'cultural filter', i.e. a motivated intervention on the ST aimed at adjusting the translation in terms of the usage norms and the stylistic conventions prevalent in the TL community. Covert translation is opposed by House to **overt translation**, thus resulting in one of the many distinctions that can ultimately be traced back to the German theologian Friedrich Schleiermacher's identification of two general approaches to translating a text: *Verfremdung*, or moving the TL reader towards the SL author, and *Entfremdung,* or moving the SL author towards the TL reader (see also **domestication** and **foreignization,** and **documentary** and **instrumental translation**). House's distinction, in particular, is proposed as part of a theory of translation **assessment**; as stressed by Hatim (2001: 96), it has played a pioneering role in guiding the attention of scholars towards issues such as the nature of the relationship between ST and TT, the way texts relate to their users and the difference between what is and what is not 'translation' (see also **Juliane House** in the 'Key Thinkers' section).

Creativity

Creativity is often considered as one of the aspects of translation seen as problem-solving, thus in relation not only to the translation of genres commonly identified as involving 'creative writing' (e.g. fiction and poetry) but also to the translation of any text that poses some kind of problem to the translator (see **translation problem**). A creative strategy may therefore be characterized as one that helps the translator to overcome the problem represented by a particular ST element for which no automatic TL solution is provided. Kussmaul (1995: Chap. 2) discusses hypotheses on how creative translation solutions are achieved through the deployment of various strategies, showing in particular how the translator can overcome a 'blockage problem' by changing strategies. For example, he observes translation trainees faced with the translation of the following phrase (taken from a magazine article): . . . *fanned by the flattery of murmuring machos* (said of someone who is on holidays, sitting on an exotic beach) and notes how the translation into German proposed by some trainees (. . . *umschmeichelt von bewundernden Blicken*, or 'caressed by admiring looks') is arrived at by what he calls 'divergent thinking', i.e. in this case looking for a translation of the word 'machos' on the basis of a different feature than that of HUMAN BEING (Kussmaul 1995: 42). Using a completely different analytical frame, Kenny (2001) shows how a **parallel corpus** can be used first to locate examples of single-word and collocational creativity in STs and then to check how these elements have been handled in translation.

Cultural studies approaches

Generally speaking, scholars looking at translation from the perspective of cultural studies are interested in the social and cultural conditions under which translations, and especially literary translations, are produced (see Bassnett [1980] 2002; Bassnett and Lefevere 1990). In particular, they look at the values which motivate the decisions taken by translators (especially values of an ideological, political and ethical nature), investigate the effects that these decisions have on texts, their readers and the cultures in which they are produced, and examine aspects such as identity and conflict as emerging in the work of translators in different historical periods or in given societies. While scholars working within the tradition of **descriptive translation studies** generally refrain from making evaluative judgements on translated texts, some scholars examining translation within a cultural studies approach can often be seen to take an activist stance, suggesting for instance that translators take on a more visible role than they are accustomed to (cf. Venuti [1995] 2008; Tymoczko 2007). Such attitudes sometimes translate into new forms of prescriptivism inspired by a programme of social and ideological change merging the study and practice of translation.

See also: **cultural turn, culture, ideology, power**.

Cultural turn

The so-called 'cultural turn' is an attempt at moving the study of translation from a more formalist approach to one that laid emphasis on extra-textual factors related to cultural context, history and convention. The scholars who promoted it (see especially Bassnett and Lefevere 1990) felt that the study of translation should embrace the tools of cultural history and cultural studies and start asking new questions having to do, for instance, with the role translation plays in shaping literary systems, the **power** negotiations translators are involved in and the status of translated texts as rewritings of the originals. Attention to such questions had already emerged in the work of the scholars associated with **Polysystem Theory** in the 1970s (see also **descriptive translation studies**). In the intervening years, the attention of many more scholars coming from different traditions has turned to questions related to **culture** and the related realms of **ideology** and **ethics** (see **cultural studies approaches**). This has marked a generalized shift away from source-oriented to target-oriented theories. Outside the field of literary translation, other scholars have followed a similar path, moving from source-focused approaches to theories that emphasized the role of social and cultural factors operating in the target environment. *Skopos* **theory** and other **functionalist approaches** have been pioneers in this respect.

Culture

Culture is a much debated notion in terms of both its definition and its significance for the practice and study of translation. A simplistic definition of culture based on the way it has traditionally been considered by translation scholars might see it as that dimension which is linked to the knowledge, activities and artefacts associated with a given language community and which provides added meaning to the basic linguistic, referential meaning of words. Various procedures have been identified for the interlinguistic transfer of such meaning, each implying greater or lesser degrees of meaning loss. Some particular linguistic items are traditionally presented as **culture-bound terms**, i.e. as having a meaning that is particularly closely associated with a given culture. More recently, largely as a consequence of the **cultural turn** experienced in translation studies, the role of culture has been reassessed and its significance for both the practice and the study of translation is felt by some scholars (e.g. Snell-Hornby 1988; Bassnett and Lefevere 1990) to be a central concern of the field.

Adopting a perspective derived largely from anthropology, Katan (2004: 26) defines culture as 'a shared mental model or map of the world', or a 'system of congruent and interrelated beliefs, values, strategies and cognitive environments which guide the shared basis of behaviour'. In such a view, culture forms a hierarchical system in which three fundamental levels can be identified: a 'technical' level, a 'formal' level and an 'informal or out-of-awareness' level, each progressing towards the more hidden, unquestioned assumptions that individuals in a culture share about the world and their own identities. The 'technical' level is the visible part of culture, the one corresponding to the traditional view mentioned above. It is the level at which culture is acquired through explicit instruction, the one concerning artefacts, concepts and ideas; linguistically, this is the level at which culture-bound terms operate. It is mostly at this level that translation theory has traditionally attempted to describe types and degrees of equivalence and ways of securing them in translation. The second, 'formal' level of culture is that of shared practices; it echoes H. J. Vermeer's (1986) definition of culture as everything that should be known, mastered and felt in order to assess if members of a given society are behaving acceptably or deviantly in their various roles (quoted in Snell-Hornby 2006: 55). Linguistically, this is the level of patterns of practices variously seen as genres or text types. It is also the level at which recent notions proposed by translation studies such as **norms** and *skopos* (see ***skopos* theory**) can be seen to operate. The third level, that of 'informal' culture, is the invisible layer of culture, the one at which individuals operate out of awareness. It comprises the unquestioned core values and beliefs that guide cultural choices at the formal level and are acquired through 'inculcation' via family, school and the media. At this level, culture can be seen to echo a notion which has recently acquired centrality in translation studies adopting a sociological slant, that of ***habitus***. This view of culture as a triadic, hierarchical system is essentially aimed at providing a more comprehensive view of its role in translation. In so doing, it is also meant to provide conceptual support both to translator training and to attempts at raising the professional status of translators as mediators between languages *and* cultures.

A slightly different view of culture and its significance in translation is proposed by **cultural studies approaches**, which adopt a more activist stance in their attempts at rendering the role of translators more visible. In general, these approaches emphasize the social and ideological pressures urging individuals to conform to established practices and see culture not so much as a set of levels but as an integrated system through which text meanings are to be negotiated. On this basis, both individuals and texts cannot be assigned to one culture in particular but are seen to have various allegiances, some of which can be brought to bear on translation questioning the prevailing norms (as is proposed, for instance, by feminist theories of translation and **postcolonial approaches**). Seen from this angle, culture has close links to issues of **power**: translators intervene between competing power systems that are often unequal; they are no longer impartial mediators but agents of social change (Tymoczko 2007) or activists (Baker 2006).

Culture-bound terms

These are terms or expressions referring to elements or concepts that are closely associated with a certain language and culture, e.g. *sarong* in Malay, *tortilla* or *siesta* in Spanish, *five o' clock tea* in English and other terms referring to geography, traditions, institutions and technologies (a synonym for 'culture-bound terms' that is perhaps most common in some non-English speaking countries is *realia*). Various techniques are employed for the translation of such elements, depending on whether the audience is already familiar with the term or concept, or the possibility to find functional equivalents in the TL, i.e. terms that refer to analogous concepts in the TL culture. So, for example, some terms are translated by **borrowing** (where necessary with transliteration), e.g. *Weltanschauung* from German or *samovar*, transliterated from Russian. Others are translated by **calque**, e.g. English *Prime Minister*, Italian *Primo Ministro*. In other cases a functional equivalent may be provided, e.g. *Abitur* in German for English *A-levels*, or the SL item may be retained and a short explanation added, e.g. *the Daily Telegraph* translated into Italian as *il quotidiano Daily Telegraph* (where *quotidiano* is 'daily newspaper').

Denotative meaning

The denotative, or referential, meaning of a linguistic expression is its stable, abstract meaning independent of the context and situation. It is usually contrasted with **connotative meaning**, which is the emotive, subjectively variable component of meaning. For example, the word *night* has the denotative meaning of 'a period of darkness between sunset and sunrise' but can also be associated with connotative meanings relating to scariness or loneliness.

Descriptive translation studies

The term is today used as a general label for those approaches to the study of translation that start from an interest in translation as it actually occurs and as part of cultural history. The label 'Descriptive Translation Studies' was originally used by the scholar James S. Holmes in a paper delivered in 1972 but published much later (in Holmes 1988) to indicate one of the branches of translation studies as a discipline of scientific inquiry. Holmes thought that, much as what happens in other scientific fields, the theoretical branch of the discipline should draw on a substantial body of results coming from genuinely descriptive studies, i.e. observations of what translations are like, how they are produced and how they affect the cultural contexts in which they emerge. This was a deliberate attempt at moving away from the prescriptive attitude that was previously found in many studies of translation, which were aimed primarily at either formulating rules and guidelines for the practice and evaluation of translation or at developing instruments for translator training – tasks that Holmes saw as belonging to a third branch of the discipline, 'Applied Translation Studies', falling outside the scope of pure research.

Holmes' ideas initially circulated, in the 1970s, among a restricted number of scholars (including Gideon Toury, Itamar Even-Zohar, Anton Popovič and André Lefevere) who, in the next two decades, gradually developed and propagated them. The term 'descriptive translation studies' has today come to indicate the work of these and the other scholars (such as José Lambert and Theo Hermans) who have consolidated and expanded this tradition of research (also referred to with other labels such as 'systemic approach' or 'Manipulation school'). In general, the various approaches to the study of translation adopted by these scholars can be said to share an interest in the following aspects (Hermans 1985: 10–11; see also Hermans 1999: 31–45): the **norms** governing the production and reception of translations (Toury 1995; Chesterman 1997); the relation between translation and other types of text production; the role and place of translations within a given culture. Translations are seen primarily as empirical facts of the target culture, which implies that research on translation should start not from the STs but with the translated texts (hence the more general label of 'target-oriented approaches' sometimes used for this body of research). In the target culture, translations are seen as part of a complex system of texts and expectations, which often implies abandoning the attention traditionally paid to the relationship between translation and original, especially as seen in terms of **equivalence**. The constraints acting on the activity of translators are seen to be not only of a linguistic but also of an aesthetic, economic and ideological nature. Describing these constraints is seen by scholars working in this tradition as a fundamental task of translation studies and one which, in line with Holmes' initial proposal, can provide the basis for the explanations and predictions put forward at a theoretical level.

While descriptive translation studies have traditionally focused their attention on questions related to the production, reception and impact of translations (and especially literary translations) from a sociocultural or historical perspective, more recent lines of inquiry based on empirical approaches include the cognitive and behavioural aspects of the process of translation at individual level and the development of translation **competence** (see **process-oriented research**).

See also: **Polysystem Theory**.

Deverbalization

The term refers to the idea that a translator or interpreter should move away from the surface structure (the 'verbal' expression) of the ST, thus arriving at the intended meaning of the text to be expressed in the target language. It is often presented as a way of avoiding formal **interference** of the source language or text. The term is associated with the *Théorie du sens* elaborated, with reference to interpreting, by Danica Seleskovitch (1976) and other scholars of the so-called Paris School (see also **interpretive approach**).

Difficulty

Difficulty in translation can be characterized as the question of 'what makes a text difficult to translate'. Answers to this question are bound, more often than not, to receive relative answers, as the sources and nature of the difficulty attached to a given source text or, more generally, to a translation task may be seen to vary according to a number of diverse factors and to the particular types of **translation problem** the text presents. First, a text may be difficult to translate because of the particular pair of languages involved. Some researchers (e.g. Hale and Campbell 2002) have looked at whether the same text can be equally difficult to translate into typologically different languages. In other words, they looked at whether the difficulty emerging in the translation from English to a given TL (Spanish) is of the same nature as that emerging in relation to another, maybe very distant TL (say, Arabic). Their findings suggest that English ST items such as words low in propositional content and complex nouns phrases are difficult to translate irrespective of the target language.

Linked to this is the question whether translation difficulty is related to features of the ST (e.g. compound nouns in English STs) or to TL aspects (e.g. lexical *lacunae*, or gaps, with respect to certain ST items). Another factor difficulty can be linked to is the level of **competence** of the translator. A given text or task may turn out to be particularly difficult for novice translators but be considered relatively easy by more experienced translators. The reason for such different responses to difficulty may be seen to lie not only in the better TL skills of experienced translators but also in the fact that their experience makes them better equipped to face difficulties related to the subject matter of the ST and to the **genre** conventions applying in the two languages involved. The perception of difficulty may also vary between less and more experienced translators, as the former may, for instance, be more preoccupied with questions of lexical equivalence while the latter are more interested in ensuring functional or genre equivalence between the ST and TT. Other potential sources of difficulty, which may or may be not related to the above aspects, include the translators' background, their emotional involvement in the task and their ability in using reference materials. In short, labelling a given ST as inherently difficult for translation purposes is no straightforward matter as the extent and nature of the difficulty it poses may vary according to a series of often interrelated factors. A distinction between the two notions of translation difficulty and translation problem is found in Nord (1991, 1997), where problems are seen as objectively identified phenomena of a textual, pragmatic, cultural or linguistic nature while difficulties are characterized as a subjective phenomenon that depends on the individual translator (or translation trainee) and arises because of 'deficient linguistic, cultural or translational competence' or because of a lack of 'appropriate documentation' (Nord 1997: 64). In particular, Nord (1991: 151–155) distinguishes between four types of difficulties: (1) those depending on the degree of comprehensibility of the source text; (2) those depending on the translator; (3) those related to the nature of the translation task and (4) those related to the specificity of the subject matter.

The distinction between problem and difficulty, however, is not always clear-cut. It is true that in some cases an element of the SL seems to be objectively problematic, i.e. likely to be a source of difficulty for translators in whatever type of text the element appears and for whatever reason the text is translated. So-called **culture-bound terms** seem to be a case in point. However, in many other cases the distinction does not take into account such crucial aspects as the level of competence of translators. Translator-specific 'difficulties' are taken by Nord (1991: 153) to exist even for experienced translators, in which case they can often hardly be distinguished from 'objective' problems – if not precisely for the level of competence of the translators the researcher is observing (and this, in turn, is not easy at all to define with absolute objectivity).

Directionality

The term refers to the direction of translation in terms of the two languages involved, a distinction usually being made between translation from a foreign language into one's mother tongue, or direct translation, and translation from one's native language into a foreign language, or **inverse translation**. Direct translation is generally considered to be the ideal or standard situation for professional translators, but in actual practice translation is often carried out into a non-mother tongue. This happens, for example, when in a particular market not enough mother-tongue translators are available, or when translated texts having an eminently informative purpose (especially texts translated into English) are addressed to an international audience.

Documentary translation

The term refers to both a method and a type of translation having as their primary aim that of reporting on the communication given in the original text (Nord 1991). A documentary translation can be seen as a reproduction of the ST which privileges formal correspondence, or a way of informing the reader of the content of the ST without fitting the TT to the target situation in either functional or communicative terms. In Nord (1991), documentary translation is contrasted with **instrumental translation**.

Domestication

Domestication is a global strategy of translation aimed at producing a transparent, fluent style in the TL. For Venuti ([1995] 2008), this strategy is concerned both with the mode of linguistic and stylistic transfer chosen for foreign texts and with the choice of texts to be translated. As a mode of translation, domestication entails translating in a transparent form felt as capable of giving access to the ST author's precise meaning. This in turn influences the choice of texts to be translated, as these are selected largely for their capacity to be translated with a domesticating approach. Venuti sees domestication as involving an ethnocentric reduction of the ST to TL values and opposes it to the alternative strategy of **foreignization**.

Dubbing

Lip-synchronized dubbing is, together with **subtitling**, the dominant form of language transfer in **audiovisual translation**, especially as regards films and TV fiction. It consists in replacing the original voice track with the voices of dubbing actors speaking in the TL, recreating the delivery pace of the original voices and synchronizing the TL voice track with the lip movements of the characters on screen (the term dubbing is also used to describe the re-recording of voices in the same language, e.g. to enhance the quality of the voice track). Translation of the dialogue is performed on a written copy of the film script and then handed over to a 'dialogue writer' that identifies potential problems in terms of synchronization. Once the translation has been adapted, revoicing in the TL is recorded by actors under the supervision of a dubbing director and a sound engineer. The presence of various professionals in the dubbing process makes it a more expensive form of audiovisual translation than subtitling.

Compared to subtitling, dubbing allows viewers to watch a foreign film with less processing effort, conveys more of the original dialogue or speech and allows a better reproduction of interactional dynamics between the characters. It is, however, a time-consuming and expensive process if compared to either subtitling or the other forms of **revoicing**. From a linguistic and cultural point of view, dubbing is seen to impose limits on the naturalness of the translated text and to frequently involve the neutralization of socio-linguistic variation portrayed by the SL dialogue.

Dynamic equivalence

For Nida (1964; see also Koller 1979: 187–191), this is a mode of translation in which the message of the original text is transported into the TL in such a way that the response of TL receivers is essentially the same as that of the original text receivers. Dynamic equivalence is based on the principle of **equivalent effect** and is contrasted by Nida with 'formal' equivalence. As an example, Nida (1964: 159–160) quotes, from J. B. Phillips' translation of the New Testament' the rendering of *philemati agioi* (literally, 'greet one another with a holy kiss') with 'give one another a hearty handshake' (see also **Eugene A. Nida** in the 'Key Thinkers' section). Venuti ([1995] 2008: 16–18) provides a critical discussion of the concept, centred around the idea that for the response of the TL receiver to be considered essentially similar to that of the SL receiver, linguistic and cultural differences are not to be seen as constitutive of meaning.

Empirical studies of translation

The term refers to the studies of translation based on observable data and carried out according to a scientific method of inquiry, i.e. one based on the testing of hypotheses (cf. Chesterman 1993, 1997; Toury 1995). Empirical studies can be both process and product oriented and are centred essentially around two sets of questions. On the one hand, they try to describe what goes on in the translator's mind as he or she is performing the translation task. In doing so, these studies make hypotheses on those elements pertaining to either the text or the context which lead translators to go beyond automatic or routine TL solutions and necessitate a problem-solving or decision-making approach (see also **process-oriented research**). Other studies are centred on translation as product and aim at a description of the regularities observed in translated texts, so as to identify either the **norms** adhered to by a given community of translators or the so-called **universals of translation** (see also **product-oriented research**). Both approaches are concerned with the identification of the strategies deployed by translators, either to achieve certain goals or in response to what they (or the researchers) perceive to be the problems found in the source texts or related to any other aspect of a given translation task (see **translation problem**). Note that the label 'empirical' has sometimes been used to describe what are otherwise known as **descriptive translation studies**.

Empowerment

In the context of translator training, empowerment is seen by Kiraly (2000) as the emancipation of students from teacher-centred models of education. This is presented by Kiraly as part of a wide-ranging programme aimed at 'transferring the responsibility of learning to the learners, individually and collectively' (Kiraly 2000: 18). Within such a programme, teachers should act as guides or consultants rather than distributors of knowledge and students should experience real or simulated translation activities. The term is also used in Tymoczko (2007),

where it is related to the broader socio-cultural and ideological implications of translation. In particular, 'empowering' translators means,
for Tymoczko, liberating them from the constraints imposed by dominant Western views on translation and rendering them fully aware of
'the ideological functions of the processes and products of translation'
(2007: 44). On this basis, translators should be capable of exercising
their **agency** (i.e. their ability to take conscious decisions) at every
level of the translation process – from the global decisions related to
which texts to translate down to micro-level decisions regarding, for
instance, how foreign names should be represented or transliterated.

Equivalence

Equivalence is the term used to refer to the relationship existing
between a translation and the original text, a relationship that has
been observed by scholars from a wide variety of perspectives. Often
presented as a central concern for those who study translation, equivalence is also perhaps the most problematic and divisive issue in the
field of translation studies. Following Halverson (1997), the different
weight given to a discussion of equivalence can be taken as one of the
lines of demarcation between two general approaches to translation:
the linguistically oriented approach that was prevalent in the 1960s
and 1970s and the historical-descriptive approach that emerged during the 1970s and today represents, in its various incarnations, one of
the dominant paradigms in the field.

Equivalence can be seen as a relationship of 'sameness' or 'similarity',
which however leads to the problems of 'establishing relevant units of
comparison, specifying a definition of sameness, and enumerating relevant qualities' (Halverson 1997: 210). In other words, once two texts are
described as equivalent, it remains to be seen: (1) at what level equivalence is established (is it morphemes, words, sentences or whole texts?);
(2) how sameness or similarity is defined (and to what degree it holds);
and (3) in terms of what specific traits or qualities two texts can be said
to be the same or similar (is it meaning, context or function?). Different
scholars have provided different answers to these questions, while some

theorists have tended to reject or ignore them altogether: Snell-Hornby (1988: 22) sees equivalance as an 'unsuitable' concept, while Hans J. Vermeer's *skopos* **theory**, in considering translation as essentially dependent on its purpose and its situation in the target culture, makes the definition of translation as providing an 'equivalent' for the ST ultimately immaterial.

The linguistic approach has traditionally assigned equivalence a primary role, making it its principal object of study and using it to differentiate translation from other forms of derivative text production (e.g. summarization). Scholars following this approach see TL texts or items as relatable to certain aspects of the original text. In so doing they presuppose a *tertium comparationis* for the textual material in the languages involved in translation. Catford (1965) sees equivalence as leading to the replacement of SL items with TL items belonging to the same category or, by the operation of translation **shifts**, to a different category that expresses the same meaning in the text at hand. Introducing a socio-linguistic perspective, Nida (1964; see also Nida and Taber 1969) starts to focus on the qualities which define equivalence and makes a distinction between 'formal' and 'dynamic' equivalence (see **Eugene A. Nida** in the 'Key Thinkers' section). A detailed treatment of the aspects in terms of which equivalence can be characterized (see point 3 above) can be found in Koller (1979), where, accommodating insights from pragmatics, various levels at which equivalence obtains are identified: *formal, denotative, connotative, pragmatic* and *text-normative* (i.e. based on the norms and conventions characterizing a particular text type). In general, the main object of study of the scholars adopting a linguistic approach is the relationship between source and target, which some of them (e.g. Wilss 1982) investigate following a 'scientific' programme of research, i.e. one aimed at defining the 'essence' of translation (see **essentialism**). It is, however, already evident in Nida's and Koller's work that equivalence should be seen not in absolute but in relative terms.

The notion of equivalence was 'turned on its head' (Hatim 2001: 69) by **Polysystem Theory** and other historical-descriptive approaches. Rather than assuming the existence of transfer norms between languages, scholars following these approaches see the choice of equivalents as governed by socio-cultural norms, literary conventions and other factors having to do with the presuppositions regarding relevance and the nature of the end-product. As all of these various factors really have to do with the target language/culture, in some descriptive approaches the notion of equivalence has come to be replaced by that of **norms** and talk of linguistic or even functional equivalence is deemed irrelevant. The empirical nature of the analyses carried out by these scholars, engaged as they are in identifying the features of target systems that are relevant for describing translations, is at odds with a clearly delineated definition of equivalence.

With a much more restricted sense, 'equivalence' is the label used by Vinay and Darbelnet ([1958] 1995) for a specific translation procedure whereby a conventional equivalent expression is provided for a given ST segment, as is typically the case with idioms.

Equivalent effect

The term refers to the principle that Nida (1964: 159) sees as the basis of **dynamic equivalence** in translation. A translation, in other words, should strive to produce the same or similar effect in the TL readers as that produced by the ST on the SL readers. The notion of equivalent effect has been criticized on the grounds that translation invariably involves a loss of the meanings and context associated with the ST and that response to a text is hardly the same in two different cultures and times.

Essentialism

A view of science as the pursuit of knowledge about the 'essence' of things, i.e. what things are in themselves and not in relation to how different observers see them. This view dates back to the Aristotelian view of concepts as having specific and distinctive properties and is ultimately grounded in logical empiricism. The difference between the various approaches to the study of translation (particularly with reference to what translation 'is' or 'does') is sometimes presented in terms of the two extreme positions of *essentialism* and *non-essentialism* (cf. Halverson 1997), the former claiming that meanings are objective and stable and that the task of translators is to find such meanings and transfer them, the latter viewing meanings as inherently non-stable and always subject to interpretation. In general, essentialism tends to be associated with empirical or descriptive approaches to translation while non-essentialism is seen as characteristic of postmodern, **cultural studies approaches**. Between the two extremes, however, there are many intermediate positions. For example, the strictly objective view of translation associated with some linguistically oriented approaches of the 1960s and 1970s has been abandoned by the more relativist positions held by **descriptive translation studies**. In general, although the various approaches to translation leaning towards essentialism or non-essentialism may continue to appear difficult to reconcile, especially as regards the role to be attributed to empirical observation, there is today some agreement between scholars that any definition of translation is closely associated with the theory adopted to observe it and that whatever data are employed to study translation they are not neutral with respect to theory. An attempt at establishing a 'shared ground' between different approaches to translation is presented in an article by Chesterman and Arrojo (2000) in the journal *Target*, which was followed by a debate between various other scholars in the subsequent issues of the journal.

Ethics

Ethical considerations can be seen to apply to various aspects of translation, ranging from questions of professional practice to issues such as the role of translators in fostering intercultural communication or in appropriately representing SL authors' ideas. Following Chesterman (2001), four main strands can be identified in the way translation scholars have discussed the ethics of translation. The first (labelled *ethics of representation* by Chesterman) is the particular preoccupation of some theorists with translation as a representation of the

Other. A line of thought starting from Friedrich Schleiermacher in the 19th century and continuing more recently with Berman (1984) and Venuti (1998 [1995] 2008) sees translation as always involving interpretation and thus inevitably inserting TL values and beliefs liable to distort the representation of the Other contained in original texts. The translator's ethical dilemma has thus to do with how to choose an interpretation of the original text that minimizes this distortion. The second strand (*ethics of service*) is related to translation as a commercial service supplied to a client and concerns the identification of the practices that best serve the requirements of the **translation brief** as agreed between translator and client. This is the particular aspect of ethics considered (largely implicitly) in **functionalist approaches** (see also **loyalty**). A third strand (*ethics of communication*) sees translation as generally aimed at fostering intercultural communication and treats the translator's performance of a mediating role between people or cultures as an essentially ethical question. This is the approach taken, for instance, by Pym (2000), who sees translators as acting in an ethically appropriate way when their translations optimize cooperation. Finally, the fourth strand (*norm-based ethics*) is linked to views of translation as a norm-governed activity (see **norms**): in this perspective, behaving ethically means behaving in accordance with the norms that expect translators to provide translations that can be trusted as truthful representations of original texts.

Evaluation, see **assessment**.

Expertise

For Chesterman (1997) expertise is the last stage in the acquisition of translation skills (see **competence**), and in particular the stage at which translation is performed largely as automatic, intuitive action. Kiraly (2000: 30) defines expertise as 'the competence to accomplish translation tasks to the satisfaction of clients and in accordance with the norms and conventions of the profession with respect to producing a translated text *per se*'. This is distinguished from *professionalism*

(Kiraly 2000: 31), which has to do with the deontological aspects of the profession, such as the commitment to meet deadlines and the charging of appropriate fees.

Explicitation

The term refers to the phenomenon whereby a translated text is seen to convey information in a more explicit form than in the original text, for example by adding connectives or explanatory phrases. This can be seen either as the result of a conscious **translation technique** used by the translator (as in Vinay and Darbelnet [1958] 1995) or as a tendency inherent in translated texts. The observation of such tendency has led some scholars to formulate the so-called *explicitation hypothesis* (first proposed by Blum-Kulka 1986), which claims that translators universally tend to make things more explicit, linguistically, in the TT than they are in the ST. Compared to other **universals of translation**, this claim has received so far the most attention by researchers. It is based on the observation of how translators treat aspects such as ambiguity and unclear structures in the ST, how they use pronouns and connectives or how they tend to add explanations to obscure and **culture-bond terms** found in the ST. Care should be taken, however, in interpreting a given feature as an instance of explicitation, as other factors (such as the temporal or cultural distance between the languages involved) may have played a role in the process of translation (Mauranen 2007: 39).

Fluency

The term refers to the idea that a translated text should read like an original and not be recognizable as a translation. In relation to literary translation, Venuti ([1995] 2008) sees fluency as an ideal and deplores the way in which it has dominated the Anglo-Saxon translation tradition; he maintains that this ideal has entailed the invisibility of the translator in the translation of literary works. In order to be more visible, Venuti argues, translators should resist the temptation to produce fluent target texts because such texts deceive readers into thinking that they are originals. Ultimately, fluency, by making the translator invisible, denies the source culture and its right to appear as something different. It is therefore an unethical choice and to it Venuti opposes a resistant way of translating that is more ethical for both the translator and the source culture (see **ethics**). This way of translating may entail using more marked, unusual TL forms, archaisms, mixed registers and other aspects that might allow the 'otherness' of the original text to be felt by TL readers.

See also: **domestication, foreignization**.

Foreignization

The term refers to a translation strategy aimed at rendering the ST conspicuous in the target text or, in other words, at avoiding the **fluency** that would mask its being a translation (which can be seen as the result of the opposite strategy of **domestication**). The term is mostly associated with the name of Lawrence Venuti ([1995] 2008) who, largely in relation to the translation of literary and philosophical works, sees TL fluency as an ideal that suppresses the 'otherness' of the source text and minimizes the role of the translator. Foreignizing translation is thus seen by Venuti as a form of *resistant translation* opposing the prevailing ethnocentric modes of transfer. For Venuti foreignizing translation is not to be equated with **literal translation**. He allows this strategy of translation to take very different, even conflicting forms: not only close, resistant renderings, but also renderings that mix different cultural discourses, or even ones that are free and fluent. The two concepts of 'domestication' and 'foreignization' must be seen as showing contingent variability, meaning that their definition always depends on the specific historical and cultural situation in which a translation is made (see Venuti [1995] 2008: 19–20); see also **Lawrence Venuti** in the 'Key Thinkers' section.

Free vs literal translation

This is the binary opposition that has dominated the debate on translation over the centuries. Free translation is usually taken to concentrate on conveying the meaning of the ST disregarding the formal or structural aspects of the ST. Literal translation is normally taken to be a mode of translation that remains close to the form of the original.

'Literal' is an ambiguous term. It could mean *word-for-word*, i.e. a translation which gives priority to lexical correspondences and results in ungrammatical sentences, or it could also mean a translation that is as close as possible to the original while still ensuring TL grammaticality (but not naturalness). Barkhudarov (1993; quoted in Chesterman 1997: 12) correlates the free/literal opposition with the choice of the **unit of translation**, so that the smaller the unit, the more literal the result, and the larger the unit, the freer the result. Thinkers and scholars have had different views on the merits or disadvantages of literalness. Newmark (1981: 39) believes that literal translation should always be preferred where possible and 'provided that equivalent effect is secured' (see **equivalent effect**). Robinson (1991: 153), on the other hand, argues that the only valid criterion for translation is that the ST and the TT 'should stand in some way of recognizable relation to each other', a position that seems to reject the idea of **equivalence** and therefore the free/literal polarity altogether.

As regards free translation, this is sometimes taken to mean *sense-for-sense* translation but it has been seen as taking a variety of forms depending on the exact nature of the type (or types) of translation it is opposed to (cf. Robinson 1991, 1998). In fact, following the tripartite distinction proposed by Jerome in the 4th century AD, free translation has often been distinguished from both word-for-word and sense-for-sense translation, where free translation is usually presented as being 'unfaithful' to the text, or a bad translation. This tripartite distinction is again found in John Dryden's differentiation between *metaphrase* (word-for-word translation), *paraphrase* (sense-for-sense translation) and *imitation*, which is defined as a translation that takes on very general hints from an original. As pointed out by Robinson (1998: 88–89) free translation, whatever it is opposed to, remains a difficult notion to define and probably the best way of characterizing it is to see it as translation that deviates from the 'hegemonic norms' that establish, in a given period or community, what faithful translation is. Thus, where faithful is equated with sense-for-sense, a free translation will be one that takes greater liberties with the ST, but where the dominant norm sees faithful translation as word-for-word, then sense-for-sense will be seen as a form of free translation.

Functionalist approaches

This is a general label for those approaches that see translation as an act of communication and a form of action involving not only linguistic but also social and cultural factors. These approaches place particular emphasis on the *function* of the target text (hence the label), which they see as the essential factor in determining how choices are made in translating. They are also characterized by their detailed consideration of real-life scenarios of professional translation, which they take to be a fundamental aspect in providing theoretical descriptions of translation.

Theories and models associated with functionalist approaches include **skopos theory** and the model of **translatorial action**, both developed (independently at first) in the late 1970s and early 1980s. These theories can be seen as part of the **cultural turn** that was taking place in translation studies at the time (cf. Snell-Hornby 2006: Chap. 2). Besides Hans J. Vermeer, who developed the *skopos* theory, the group of scholars usually associated with functionalist approaches includes Hans Hönig, Paul Kussmaul and Christiane Nord (see Hönig and Kussmaul 1982; Nord 1991, 1997), all of them from Germany. Historically, their work emerged as a reaction to the linguistically oriented approaches prevalent up to the

1970s, which saw translation as a process of transfer largely independent from the specific situation of the TT in a given socio-cultural setting. To this, functionalism opposed a view of texts as embedded in, and shaped by, the setting in which they are produced. Particular importance is attached to the function served by a TT in its environment, which may or may not coincide with the function of the ST ('functional constancy' is seen as by these approaches as the exception rather than the rule). In any case, whether it coincides with ST function or not, TT function is always seen as the overriding factor in determining the choices made during the translation process.

Functionalist approaches share the emphasis on the target-environment and on the importance of social factors with other approaches that emerged in the same years, particularly **descriptive translation studies**. The two approaches, however, differ in their fundamental aims and in the treatment of central notions such as 'function' and **'culture'** (see Snell-Hornby 2006: 63–67). A functionalist approach such as *skopos* theory seeks to provide a general account of translation, thereby touching on problems of an applied nature such as translation assessment and translator training; also, it does not refrain from evaluative judgements. Descriptive translation studies, on the other hand, generally stick to descriptive accounts and programmatically reject any form of evaluation. As regards more specific notions, 'culture' is seen by descriptive approaches in the more abstract sense of a systemic background, whereas functionalism sees culture as operating both at social and individual level. As for 'function', again this is considered by descriptive approaches as an abstract 'value' assigned to an item by the 'network of relations' it establishes within a system (Toury 1995: 12). Functionalism sees the function of a text in more operational terms, looking not so much at large-scale social systems but at local social networks, and pointing to the consequences they have on the way translations are carried out and evaluated. In particular, it is in functionalist approaches that the role of people such as the commissioners of translation jobs has first been explicitly acknowledged and that translation has first been presented as governed by social interactions and extra-textual factors.

Gender

In recent years, an increasing number of studies have looked at the links between translation practice and theory on the one hand and issues related to gender on the other. Gender studies explore the ways in which maleness, femaleness and other gendered identities are constructed through attributes and attitudes that are culturally and historically determined. In this framework, language is seen as a manipulative tool that contributes to the formation of particular attitudes towards gender. Following the **cultural turn** of translation studies, various scholars have started to emphasize the role of the socio-cultural norms affecting the practice and theory of translation. In particular, some scholars have begun to look at such norms through the prism of gender studies, so as to describe the way in which translation is influenced by culturally determined attitudes to gender. A pioneering work in this respect is Simon (1996).

From the point of view of theory, some scholars have looked at how attitudes to gender contribute to construct the translators' identities and their willingness to suppress or manifest these identities in translated texts. Adopting an explicitly prescriptive attitude, some of these scholars call for particular methods of **overt translation** in which the identity of female translators should be rendered manifest by recourse to prefaces, explanations and footnotes, thus resisting the prevailing convention that the translator's subjective presence should not emerge in a translated text. Other scholars have critically examined the prevailing rhetoric and metaphors of the theoretical discourse on translation, exposing its frequently patriarchal attitude (as when free translations are described as *les belles infidèles*, using a feminine adjective referring to the presumed unfaithfulness of beautiful women). Starting in the mid-1990s considerations of gender issues have broadened so as to include plural gendered identities going beyond the male/female binary opposition. The translation of gay writing, for instance, has been studied by Harvey (2000), focusing on its translatability vis-à-vis the presence of a gay community in the TL.

As regards the practice and criticism of translation, the consideration of gender issues has often led to calls for interventionist approaches aimed at exposing and opposing the patriarchal attitudes often found in language usage and translational conventions. Von Flotow (1997) speaks of *feminist translation* as a practice intended to undermine such patriarchal conventions in translated texts and, in extreme cases, to deliberately make feminine elements visible (e.g. by playing with the gender endings of nouns and adjectives). As regards translation criticism, works such as the Bible have been examined with a view to restoring the ambiguities of the ST and the non-gendered nature of the labels used for the deity.

Genre

Genres can be seen as 'conventional forms of texts associated with particular types of social occasion' (Hatim and Mason 1997: 218). Examples would include textbooks, learned articles, reports, brochures and contracts. Considering the particular genre a text belongs to can be important in terms of the decisions taken during the translation process as regards the rhetorical structure and other genre-specific aspects of a text. The definition of genre given above is only one of the many available, especially in applied linguistics, which contributes to making genre a slippery concept. As far as translation is concerned, classification of texts are perhaps more commonly presented as based on the notion of text type (see **text typology**), especially as far as non-literary texts are concerned (see Trosborg 1997). However, some scholars (e.g. House 1997) see the notion of text type as too broadly defined (at least according to the way it has normally been presented) and consider genre as better equipped to capture the relations between a given individual text and the class of texts with which it shares a common communicative purpose.

There are other ways in which the notion of genre has been employed by translation scholars (cf. Hatim 2001: Chap. 11). From a cultural perspective, genre has been evoked to describe textual aspects that resist transfer into certain languages: Tymoczko (1990), for instance, shows how in the translation of *Hamlet* into some West African languages, the oral tradition of these languages resisted the transfer of some genre-related rhetorical and linguistic structures found in the original. Another way of looking at genre is to see translated texts as a genre in themselves (James 1989). In this sense a translation might be considered in terms of how closely it resembles other translations and how it is distinguished from texts that are not translations – an idea which may call to mind notions such as translation as a **third code**, **translationese** or the **universals of translation**.

Gist translation

The term usually refers to a translation aimed at giving a condensed version, or summary, of the contents of the original text.

Given/new information, see **theme/rheme**.

Globalization

In the last few years, an increasing number of studies have started to look at the effect of globalization on both the practice and the theoretical conceptualization of translation (cf. Lambert 1989; Cronin 2003; Pym 2006; Tymoczko 2007). The translation market has been greatly affected both by the emergence of new technologies that make communication between distant places increasingly easier and by the predominance of English as the international lingua franca of production. The emergence of English as a lingua franca and the concurrent increase in the demand for translation is seen by Pym (2006) as only an apparent paradox: while English has come to dominate communication in many international centres of economic production, at a local level the distribution and marketing of products increasingly requires translation. Pym (2006) sees many of today's translation situations as characterized by a 'one-to-many geometry' where the traditional picture of translation as occurring between a pair of languages (one source and one target) has been replaced by scenarios in which translation in a variety of target languages occurs

from source materials produced in English, often in an international-
ized form of English from which cultural elements have been removed
so that translation can more easily make adaptations to the local target environments. This has had profound effects on the way translation services at a commercial level are organized, as the considerable
size of such 'one-to-many' translation projects requires high levels of
hierarchical control and standardization.

See also: **agency, localization, professional translation**.

Habitus

The notion of *habitus* is defined by the French sociologist Pierre Bourdieu as a set of dispositions that characterize an individual (an 'agent') acting in a 'field', i.e. a particular area of activity with its institutions and laws of functioning. Proposed by Bourdieu to account for how the regularities of behaviour of the agents acting in a given field become established and maintained, the notion has been introduced in the debate on translation as a social practice by Daniel Simeoni, who defines *habitus* as the translator's particular mindset, 'the elaborate result of a personalized social and cultural history' (Simeoni 1998: 32; see also Inghilleri 2005). The typical translator's *habitus* is seen by Simeoni (1998: 23) as one of 'voluntary servitude', but it is argued that such a self-image can be changed little by little as individual translators become aware of their own habitual practice and experiment with new, alternative ways of carrying out their activity. Such alternatives could then be taken up by other translators, thus resulting in changes in their own *habitus*, and so on. In this way, translators could also start to question the **power** relations that govern their activity and find new forms of motivation for their work. At a local, individual level, this would imply a redirection of effort during a given translation task (so that, for instance, more time is devoted to searching for information than to polishing up the TT). At a global, social level, motivation strategies can, by strengthening the translators' self-image, lead translators to establish new **norms** of behaviour, which in turn could make sure that they are guaranteed more favourable working conditions or that the public's concept of translation changes in such a way as to reconsider the translator's role (cf. also Chesterman and Wagner 2002: 77).

See also: **agency**.

Hermeneutic motion

This is a label coined by George Steiner (1975) for his model of the act of translation, based on a view of translating as an essentially hermeneutic, or interpretative, activity aimed at an empathic understanding of the ST. In particular, Steiner identifies four stages in the hermeneutic motion. The first is *trust*, and this is the stage at which the translator surrenders to the alienness of the original text. At the second stage, that of *aggression*, the translator actively enters the text with the intention of extracting and appropriating meaning. This is then brought back at the third stage of *incorporation*, which is seen as entailing a modification and enrichment of the native context (unless translation is only meant to produce sterile mimicry). The fourth and final stage is that of *restitution*, and it is the stage at which the translator 'endeavours to restore the balance of forces, of integral presence, that appropriative comprehension has disrupted' (1975: 302).

Hybrid text

The term is used in translation studies in two senses. The first sense refers to the translated text, seen as a hybrid in that it results from a process that provides it with 'features that somehow seem "out of place"/"strange"/"unusual" for the receiving culture' (Schäffner and Adab 1997: 325). These features are the result of deliberate decisions by translators and do not derive from a lack of competence. In another sense, and in relation to the translation of postcolonial literature, the term hybrid text is used to characterize the texts written by writers from former colonies in the language of the ex-colonizers. These are seen as hybrid because of their creative exploitation of language varieties, idiolects, jargon, metaphors and other features coming from the language spoken in the former colony (as, for example, in Salman Rushdie's novels). Such texts are seen to pose particular problems in translation, particularly into standard European languages, due to their high degree of grammatical and lexical innovation and the high-density of **culture-bound terms** (see Snell-Hornby 2001).

Ideology

The link between ideology and translation has in recent years attracted the attention of many scholars, who have looked at it from various angles, but generally in terms of how ideological stances influence either the local and global decisions taken by translators or the reception of translated texts. Ideology is often seen in terms of **power** relations, either between the cultures involved in translation (see **postcolonial approaches**) or between the actors or groups who, in the target culture, exercise control over the practice of translation, e.g. institutions of various kinds, publishers and the translators themselves (see von Flotow 2000a; Munday and Cunico 2007).

Within the target pole, Lefevere (1992, 1998) sees ideology as one of the controlling factors or constraints over the work of translators of literary texts. In his definition, ideology is 'the conceptual grid that consists of opinions and attitudes deemed acceptable in a certain time, and through which readers and translators approach texts' (Lefevere 1998: 48). In particular, it is the ideology promoted by their 'patrons' (see **patronage**) that translators adhere to, choosing the strategies of text transfer that are most likely to reflect such adherence. Fawcett (1995) sees this as an oversimplification of a much less systematic process, and points to the main difficulty in the analysis of the ideological factors impinging on translation, i.e. establishing the *extent* and *form* of the translators' ideological mediation or intervention. The extent of the translator's ideological intervention is analysed from a linguistic and pragmatic point of view in Hatim and Mason (1997).

The translator's 'positionality' (von Flotow 2000b) is, in any case, a generally accepted concept: the translator is seen as writing from a specific moment and culture (or sub-culture) and often in dialogue with social and political trends of the moment, which makes an ideological slant inevitable. As an example, von Flotow (2000b) studies different English translations of the Bible carried out by women translators in different but not too distant historical periods. Although an explicit aim of the translators is to represent the ST as literally and faithfully as possible, von Flotow shows how in reality the translations are very different from one another and how such difference can be accounted for in terms of the ideological stances of the translators.

Implicature

Implicature is a notion used in **pragmatics** to refer to what speakers or writers mean as opposed to what they literally say. It is not to be confused with non-literal meaning, such as that of idiomatic expressions, which has a conventional character. Implicature refers to how people come to understand more than what is actually said, based on the **context** or situation. Baker (1992: 223–224) illustrates this difference with two examples. In the following exchange:

A: *Shall we go for a walk?*
B: *Could I take a rain check on that?*

the interpretation of B's utterance depends on knowledge of what the American idiom 'to take a rain check' means, namely 'to decline an offer or invitation but be willing to accept one at a later occasion'. In this other exchange:

A: *Shall we go for a walk?*
B: *It's raining.*

speaker A will likely consider B's comment on the weather as an answer to the question and select among the possible meanings of the answer ('No, we'd better not' or 'OK, but we'd better take an umbrella' or even 'Yes – we both like walking in the rain') by means of an implicature, that is, through an inference based on the specific context and on shared knowledge of the background situation (in this case, A's knowledge of whether B usually likes to walk in the rain or not). Implicatures are thus interpretations of utterances in which meaning is conveyed non-conventionally, i.e. not using the textual resources that would normally be understood as signalling a certain relation between two propositions (in the second example above, for instance, B's response might have been: *No, because it's raining* or *No – you know I don't like walking in the rain*).

More specifically, an implicature can be seen as arising from the flouting of what the linguist H. P. Grice calls the *Cooperative Principle*, a general principle of communication consisting of four maxims: (1) do not say too little or too much (quantity maxim); (2) tell the truth or what you think the truth is (quality maxim); (3) only say what is relevant (relevance maxim); (4) be perspicuous, brief and orderly (manner maxim). If any one of these maxims is flouted by a speaker, hearers will think that there is a good reason for it and, by implicature, they will arrive at the intended meaning. Pragmatic meaning, in other words, is created by the breaking of the maxims. To go back to the second example above, speaker A will interpret B's comment on the weather in terms of its relevance to the invitation.

Not all linguists accept the universality of Grice's maxims (which are essentially based on an observation of spoken English), but there is general agreement on the fact that, both in spoken and written mode, all languages use comparable sets of cooperative maxims and that implicature is relied upon by language users so as to arrive at the correct interpretation of meaning. The interest of such notions for translation studies can be seen to lie precisely in the way implied meaning can be seen to be expressed in different languages, possibly to achieve specific effects such as politeness or irony.

See also: **relevance theory**.

Incorrect meaning

The term refers to a **translation error** resulting from the attribution to a TL element of a sense that it does not have in the ST context in which it appears. Translating the French *une somme importante* into English as *an important sum* (as opposed to *a large amount of money*) would constitute such an error (Delisle et al. 1999: 147).

Indeterminacy of translation

The philosophical thesis of the indeterminacy of translation maintains that different translations of a sentence in a given original language can be incompatible with one another but at the same time all equally compatible with the semantically relevant facts expressed by the original sentence. In other words, the thesis maintains that, starting from one sentence in language A, two or more translations of the sentence can be provided in language B that, while being non-equivalent with each other, are nevertheless all equivalent to the original sentence. The thesis has been proposed by the American philosopher Willard V. O. Quine, who arrived at it through a thought experiment based on a case of *radical translation*, i.e. the interpretation of a completely unknown language with no historical or cultural links to the translating language (Quine 1960; see also Quine 1959). In particular, Quine imagines a field linguist coming across the member of a previously unknown tribe in the jungle. On noticing a rabbit scurrying by, the native says 'Gavagai' and the linguist starts asking what the utterance could mean. Possibilities of interpretation include 'Rabbit' or 'Lo, a rabbit' or even 'He is running fast'. To arrive at an interpretation of the utterance, the linguist can only observe the causal connections between the environment of the natives and their verbal behaviour. More specifically, he observes how the word 'gavagai' is used in various contexts and tests his interpretations against still other contexts, finally arriving at a translation. This, however, does not exclude that other, different translations/interpretations of the word 'gavagai' are possible, perhaps in contexts not yet observed by the linguist or because the stimulus conditions the utterance 'gavagai' is meant to respond to are of a different nature (i.e. because the utterance is polysemous). The thesis is thus that translation always implies a certain degree of indeterminacy, as meanings can only be interpreted with reference to actual contexts, that is, empirically. For Quine, the indeterminacy linked to translation is just a particular case of the indeterminacy associated with all interpretation of meaning, even within the same language.

Indirect translation

The term indicates the translation of a text carried out via an inter-
mediary translation in another language and not directly from the
original text (Vinay and Darbelnet [1958] 1995). Toury (1995: Chap. 7)
examines the role played by indirect translations in Hebrew literature
over the last 200 years, stressing the tolerant attitude towards them as
Hebrew literature was trying to catch up with the Western world, and
contrasting such tolerance with the currently prevalent norm which
tends to reject mediated translations.

Informationsangebot

As part of **skopos theory**, translation is seen by Vermeer (1986: 33) as
an 'offer of information' (*Informationsangebot*) in the target language
which imitates an offer of information in the source language while taking into account the functional, cultural and linguistic conditions obtaining at the target pole. Such a view implies that the information offered by
a text may differ according to the recipient of the text, given that different
recipients may have different expectations or presuppositions. As a consequence, different translations of the same TT are possible depending of
which particular 'information offer' they are designed to respond to.

Instrumental translation

The term refers to a method of translation aimed at producing a
text that, in the target context, functions independently from the ST
(Nord 1991). An instrumental translation, in other words, focuses on
the communicative purpose of the TT, which may be different from
that of the ST. Nord contrasts this method or type of translation with
documentary translation.

Interference

Interference is the phenomenon whereby the choices made by a
translator in translating a text are influenced by the linguistic make-up

of the original text at the morpho-syntactic, lexical, stylistic or typo-graphical level. In cases where such influence leads to a TL rendering which is either ungrammatical or unfit to the context or purpose of the translation, interference can be seen as a type of **translation error**, as in the translation of the German *Er ist hier seit gestern* with *He is here since yesterday* instead of *He has been here since yesterday*. At the level of style, interference can be seen as one of the factors that lead to **translationese**, or the particular style sometimes described as typical of translated texts.

See also: **laws of translation**.

Interlingual translation

A form of translation in which verbal signs are interpreted by means of other signs in a different language. It is one of the three general types of translation identified by Jakobson (1959), who sees this as 'transla-tion proper'. The other two types are **intralingual translation** and **intersemiotic translation**.

Interpretive approach

An approach to translation that applies the *Théorie du sens* (or Theory of Sense) developed, in relation to conference interpreting, by a group of scholars linked to the ESIT institute of interpretation and transla-tion in Paris. The theory, elaborated in the 1960s, emerged as a reac-tion to the linguistically oriented approaches prevalent at the time. It distinguishes *sense* from pre-established, abstract linguistic mean-ing. In particular, sense is meaning that derives from the interaction between what is actually said, the intention of the speaker, the level of shared knowledge between the interlocutors and the context in which the communication takes place. In interpreting, the sense of a text is arrived at through a process of **deverbalization**, which is then followed by re-expression in the TL (Seleskovitch 1976).

As regards written translation, particularly in relation to **pragmatic texts**, the process of translation is seen in this approach (see Delisle 1988) as involving three stages: *comprehension*, i.e. the extraction of

the ST author's intended meaning; *re-expression*, or the reconstruction of the text in the TL; and *verification*, i.e. a check on the accuracy
of the proposed TL solution. Comprehension entails an interpretative
analysis of the text. Re-expression is based on the application of styl-
istically and contextually appropriate writing techniques in the TL.
Verification is a quality check carried out on the TT 'not in relation to
the words of the original utterance [. . .] but in relation to the ideas
extracted from the message during its first interpretation' (Delisle
1988: 67).

Intersemiotic translation

A form of translation in which verbal signs are interpreted by means
of other signs belonging to a non-verbal system. It is one of the three
general types of translation identified by Jakobson (1959) – the other
two being **intralingual translation** and **interlingual translation**.
An example of intersemiotic translation would be the making of a
novel into a film.

Intralingual translation

A form of translation in which verbal signs are interpreted by means of
other signs in the same language. It is one of the three general types
of translation identified by Jakobson (1959) – the other two being
interlingual translation and **intersemiotic translation**.

Inverse translation

The term refers to translation carried out from one's native language into a foreign language. Professional translators are normally
expected to translate the other way round, i.e. from the foreign language (the language they have consciously learned, also known as
'second language') into their own native language (the language they
have inductively acquired, or 'first language'). This is taken to be an
ideal arrangement for various reasons, mainly having to do with the

translators' native-speaker language competence, their familiarity with the cognitive mapping of conceptual referents in the native language and their ability to establish inter-textual references as acquired through repeated exposure to native-language texts (Adab 2005).

In the last few years this idea has come under increasing scrutiny. Adab (2005: 227) sees an exclusive insistence on translation into the translator's first language as 'unenforceable and impracticable' on account of various factors. For example, in an era of globalized communications the number of people using English as a lingua franca has increased (e.g. in the business community) and their expectations as addressees of translated texts in English may be different from those of native speakers, meaning that they may accept translations that are informatively adequate but not completely native-like from a stylistic point of view. Adab also points out that, at a professional level, translation into the second language is already a reality in some countries for reasons linked to the requirements of the local translation market. In Finland, for instance, the lack of foreign speakers competent in Finnish forces mother-tongue Finnish translators to work into a second language as well. Adab believes that, by enhancing the use of already available technologies assisting translators (e.g. **translation memories**, **corpora** and the internet) and by arranging translation workflows so that **revision** by native speakers is ensured, translation into the second language may obtain more widespread recognition.

A study specifically devoted to literary translation into the second language is reported on in Pokorn (2005), who starts from the assumption that the prominence of translation into the first language is a construct of Western translation theory and that no convincing empirical results show that literary translation into a non-mother tongue is systematically of inferior quality.

Invisibility of the translator

Venuti ([1995] 2008) uses the term 'invisibility' to characterize the position and activity of the translator in the Anglo-American literary tradition, where translation is largely seen as a derivative form of text production and translations are thought to provide access to the precise meaning of a foreign literary work. In particular, as publishers, reviewers and readers expect a translated text to read like an original and therefore to present no linguistic or stylistic peculiarities, translators strive to secure readability and adhere to current TL usage. This leads, in readers, to the illusion of transparency and contributes to making the translators' own work invisible.

See: **fluency, domestication, foreignization**.

Keystroke logging

The term refers to the computer logging of the keyboard activity performed by the translator during a written translation task. A dedicated software tool (such as *Translog*; see Jakobsen 1999) can be used to elicit this kind of data, which can be used in **process-oriented research** on translation. In particular, the software records all the keyboard activity performed by the translator and has a replay function that can be used to observe the typing process either in real time or at a different speed. The raw data provided by such software consist of the final printout of the translation and a detailed log of the typing process. This log gives information about the timing of each keystroke, pauses, revisions, deletions, corrections and so on. When gathered for a group of subjects, such information alone can, for instance, give indications as to the process features that correlate with the quality of the target texts (assuming a suitable benchmark can be found). In other words, the researcher can verify whether the best translations are produced through a smooth text generation process (i.e. one with few revisions and deletions) or whether they are arrived at via a more uneven process characterized by frequent revisions, deletions and corrections. The replay function of the software can also be used, once the text generation phase is over, as a prompt in eliciting a retrospective report on the task. While looking at the replay of his/her text generation process, the translator can comment on his/her own work, focusing, for instance, on why certain revisions were made or why a certain structure for a TT sentence was immediately discarded. As a method of data collection on the translation process, keystroke logging may be less obtrusive than **verbal reporting** and less labour-intensive from the researcher's viewpoint.

Language functions

The models of language description centred around the notion of 'function' are based on the fundamental assumption that language is a social activity that cannot be discussed without reference to the purposes for which speakers and writers use it. The functions of a language are, in such a perspective, the various uses people make of it in different communicative situations. Meaning, according to such models, is always a function of **context**: we use a given linguistic element (a word, a phrase, a sentence, a paragraph or a whole text) because by using that element we fulfil a certain communicative purpose. This idea dates back to work carried out in the first half of the 20th century by various scholars, and especially the anthropologist Bronislaw Malinowski, the linguist J. R. Firth and the psychologist Karl Bühler. In particular, in a book originally published in 1934 called *Sprachtheorie,* Bühler identified three main macro-functions of language: the 'expressive' (*Ausdruck*), i.e. the function enabling the addresser of a message to express attitudes and emotions, the 'conative' (*Appell*), i.e. the function oriented towards the addressee of a message, and the 'referential' (*Darstellung*), i.e. the function oriented towards the extra-linguistic reality. The linguist Roman Jakobson (1960) later added three more functions to those identified by Bühler: the *phatic,* i.e. that used to establish contact (as in greetings or in conversation aimed at facilitating social relationships), the *poetic,* i.e. that oriented towards the message or its manipulation for aesthetic purposes, and the *metalinguistic,* i.e. 'language about language' or the ways in which the linguistic code focuses on itself in order to clarify or explain a given message. The six functions thus identified correspond each to one of the factors that Jakobson saw as involved in communication: addresser, addressee, context, contact, message, code. Any given text will, according to Jakobson, serve one predominant function. In literary texts, for instance, prominence is given to the poetic function.

Bühler's original three functions were used by Reiss (1971) for a classification of types of texts according to the particular function they give prominence to – her aim being that of evaluating translated texts according to how well they served the prominent function of the ST. Jakobson's six functions formed the basis for Newmark's (1981, 1988) more flexible classification of text types, again based on the idea that in any given text there is one predominant function. Whereas Reiss' intention in applying the notion of function is evaluative and retrospective, Newmark's adaptation of Jakobson's six functions has a more overtly processual nature, i.e. it leads to the elaboration of a list of guidelines aimed at solving the problems more frequently encountered in translating the text types Newmark identifies. Both in Reiss' early work and in Newmark, the notion of function is considered primarily in relation to the ST. Other approaches have taken the idea of function as a pivotal notion, but have linked it primarily to the target text (e.g. Reiss' own later work with H. J. Vermeer; see **skopos theory**).

Whether the focus was on the source or the target, a consideration of the different functions served by language has helped translation scholars move away from discussions of equivalence at micro-contextual level, leading them to adopt a perspective based on the communicative purpose of translating.

See also: **text typology**.

Laws of translation

Toury (1995) sees translational behaviour as amenable to the formulation of 'laws', i.e. theoretical formulations which state the relations observed between a set of relevant variables. Such laws are of a probabilistic nature, i.e. they are meant to state the likelihood that a particular behaviour (or linguistic realization) would occur under specified conditions, and are arrived at based on the findings provided by descriptive studies. As an illustrative example, Toury (1995: 267–279) discusses two laws, the 'law of growing standardisation' and the 'law of interference'. The former says that 'in translation, source text textmes tend to be converted into target text repertoremes' (Toury 1995: 268) or, in other words, that the textual relations observed in the original texts (e.g. an unusual collocation) tend to be replaced by translators with relations that are more habitual in the target language (e.g. a fixedcollocation).

The law of interference says that ST linguistic features tend to be transferred to the TT, with the possibility of giving rise to negative transfer, i.e. deviations from codified TL practices. Laws of translation as presented by Toury can be put in relation to another notion, that of the **universals of translation**, which has received more attention on the part of researchers (for a discussion of the two notions, see Pym 2008; see also **Gideon Toury** in the 'Key Thinkers' section).

Level shift

This is a type of translation **shift** discussed in Catford (1965) and defined as a shift occurring when an SL item at one particular level, for instance grammar, is translated with a TL item at a different level, for example lexis. Thus, in the translation of the English *This text is intended for* . . . into *Le present Manuel s'addressse à* . . . in French, the level shift occurs between the SL modifier *This* and the corresponding article plus lexical adjective in the TL: *Le present*.

Literal translation

Literal translation is a translation strategy or technique involving a choice of TL equivalents that stay close to the form of the original while ensuring grammaticality in the TL. Vinay and Darbelnet (1958) include it among their translation procedures (see **shifts**) and, as an example, quote the sentence *I left my spectacles on the table downstairs* translated into French as *J'a lassé mes lunettes sur la table en bas* (Vinay and Darbelnet [1958] 1995: 34) . Newmark (1981) sees this technique as the best option for translating texts where the form is as important as the content, such as great speeches, autobiographies and literary works; these are the kinds of text that require what he calls a **semantic translation** approach.

See also: **free vs literal translation, translation strategy, translation technique**.

Loan translation, see **calque**.

Localization

The term localization refers to the process of adapting a product to a particular local market, from a linguistic, cultural and technical point of view. The term has been originally introduced for the translation of computer software applications, which were among the first type of products to require large volumes of translations to be carried out using special engineering adjustments. Today the term localization is also frequently used in relation to the translation of web sites and other products that are based on computerized technologies (e.g. mobile phones). The term itself derives from the word 'locale', indicating the combination of cultural conventions and technical standards found in a given regional area or market (see Esselink 2003).

The linguistic adaptation of a product is essentially the translation of all its text elements. In software packages, for instance, text requiring translation is found in the user interface (e.g. menus, messages and dialogue boxes), in the product documentation (comprising the online help and printed manuals) as well as in the so-called 'collateral' materials such as product boxes and multimedia demos. Translation of such elements often implies cultural adaptation, as target texts are required to reflect conventions and situations associated with the target market. For example, in the translation of the user interface all characteristics such as character sets, page sizes, address formats, calendars and date/time formats must be adapted to the conventions and standards operating in a given local market.

From a technical point of view, localization normally requires special engineering adjustments deriving from the large volumes of text to be translated and the special character of such text, two factors that have made the integration of translation technology in localization much stronger than in other areas of professional translation. The large volumes of text to be translated require teams of translators whose work needs to be given assistance and must be reviewed for consistency. Technologies such as **translation memories** and terminology management systems (see **termbase**) help on both counts. As for the texts to be translated, they can be seen as special in two senses: on the one hand, they are often highly repetitive or, as products are updated, likely to be massively recycled, which makes them suitable for the use of translation memories; on the other, they often come in formats which require special text editors, as is typically the case with interface components or web pages.

Localization has in many ways set the operational standards which many other areas of **professional translation** have later adhered to. In particular, it is in localization that translation services have first come to be organized along industrial lines, thus turning the translation process into a production chain in which other specialized figures besides translators operate (e.g. the project managers that coordinate and assist the translators working in teams). Also, the software technologies first developed to meet the needs of localization projects (especially translation memories and terminology management systems) are now commonly used in translation projects of different kinds, where they are seen to bring benefits in terms of productivity, team-work coordination and linguistic consistency.

Loyalty

The notion of loyalty has been proposed by Nord (1991, 1997) to characterize the responsibility translators have towards their partners (SL authors, TT commissioners or TL readers) in the translational interaction. Loyalty is seen by Nord as a 'moral principle indispensable in the relationship between human beings, who are partners in a communication process'; it is 'an interpersonal category referring to a social relationship between *people*' (1997: 125; original emphasis), and it should not be confused with fidelity or faithfulness, a relationship holding between texts. Relevant questions for translators are whether their loyalty lies with ST authors or TT readers or whether loyalty must be shown primarily to the commissioners or the readers of the translated text.

LSP translation, see **specialist translation**.

Machine translation

Often abbreviated to MT, machine translation is translation performed automatically by a computer with different degrees of human involvement. A distinction is often made between MT systems that are purely automatic and systems that require human assistance (e.g. in Hutchins and Somers 1992), but the difference is increasingly blurred as most available systems require some form of human intervention. Typically, human assistance in MT is required at the stage of ST preparation (**pre-editing**) or output editing (**post-editing**). Besides those based on human intervention, further classifications of MT systems are possible, depending on the text type MT is used for or the type of end user a system is addressed to. A first distinction can thus be made between specific-purpose systems, used for specialized subject-specific texts, and general-purpose systems used for general-purpose texts (Quah 2006: 173). As regards end users, a distinction can be made between stand-alone systems used by professional translators (working as freelancers or in an organization), web-based systems for home users and non-translators, and systems installed on hand-held devices for non-translators (Quah 2006: 65). Starting from the 1990s, speech recognition technology has often been combined with MT, leading to the creation of speech-to-speech, text-to-speech and speech-to-text systems.

The so-called 'architecture' on which MT systems are based relies on different approaches (an extensive overview is given in Quah 2006: Chap. 3). First-generation systems rely on 'direct translation': SL words are replaced with TL words after morpho-syntactic changes are made based on standard contrastive differences between the languages involved. Second-generation, 'rule-based approaches' are based on a view of translation as a process involving the analysis and representation of SL meaning, based on which a TL equivalent is generated. In systems using an *interlingua*, the analysis leads to an abstract representation of syntactic and semantic information that can then be converted into various TLs. Other rule-based approaches rely, instead, on *transfer* rules that convert the SL abstract representation

into an abstract TL representation, based on which a TL is then generated. These systems require different transfer models for different
language pairs. The third generation of systems is that of 'corpus-
based approaches', which gained popularity in the early 1990s. These
systems use a reference corpus of translated texts aligned with their
STs. In particular, *statistical-based* approaches use algorithms in order
to match the new SL segments to be translated with the SL segments
and their TL equivalents contained in the corpus and then compute
the likelihood that corpus-based TL equivalents are valid TL segments
for the new text to be translated. Another corpus-based approach is
that of *example-based* MT, in which segments from the new ST are
matched with existing pairs of examples extracted from the reference
corpus; once a translation is identified for the ST segments, these are
then recombined to generate a new TT. Many of the more recent MT
systems are based on approaches that combine the various methods
described so far.

  After the enthusiasm that characterized the early days of MT
research in the 1950s, fully automatic high-quality MT is today still
seen as an unrealistic goal, but MT is already being used in many contexts where it can provide fit-for-purpose output or a cost-effective
alternative to human translators. MT and translation-oriented computerized technology in general can be described as a complex and
diverse field which see 'the involvement of a wide range of "agents"
from researchers and tool developers, through evaluators to various
end-user groups including professional translators, trainers and translation companies' (Quah 2006: 196).

Mediation

The notion may be seen to refer to the role played by translators
in serving as the medium for the transfer process that takes place
between an original and a translation. This role has been observed
and described by translation scholars adopting various perspectives. The view of translators as mediators emerges clearly with the
approaches that see translation principally in terms of communication

across languages. **Functionalist approaches** see the translator acting as a mediator between texts, and particularly between the purpose of the ST and that of the TT. Texts are thus firmly established as
the poles between which mediation occurs and translation is clearly
demarcated from contrastive analysis. A further shift in perspective can be observed in more recent views of translation adopting
a sociological approach or emphasizing the link between translation
and ideology. Hatim and Mason (1997: 147) define mediation as 'the
extent to which translators intervene in the transfer process, feeding
their own knowledge and beliefs [i.e. their ideology] into their processing of a text'. The focus of attention is, in other words, moved
from texts to people, in accordance with a trend that is particularly
visible in interpreting studies: it is in studies of the social settings
in which interpreters work that researchers have for the first time
decidedly moved their focus from translated texts to those who produce them. Recent research on translation assuming a more or less
explicit sociological slant in is also giving increasing prominence to
the role of translators as a source of explanation for translational
phenomena. The term 'mediator' is thus enjoying increasingly wider
currency among those who want to stress how interlinguistic, intercultural communication is frequently affected by, and in turn affects,
the individual and social identity of translators and interpreters (see
also **agency** and *habitus*).

Meme

The notion of meme has been introduced in translation studies by
Chesterman (1997) and Vermeer (1997), probably independently
of each other (as suggested in Snell-Hornby 2006: 76), as a way of
explaining how the concept of translation changes over time and
travels from one community or group to another. The 'meme' is a
concept originally introduced in sociobiology by Richard Dawkins; it
is a unit of cultural transmission or imitation (corresponding to an
idea, a catch-phrase, a fashion, etc.) which propagates from brain
to brain, much as genes propagate from body to body via sperm or

eggs (cf. Chesterman 1997: 5). As translation is first of all a cognitive activity but it also takes place, as an event, in a given historical, social and cultural setting, an intriguing question is whether and how, in translation, the socio-cultural environment influences the workings of the brain so that certain choices and decisions are taken instead of others. Memes have been proposed as a notion capable of establishing a link between the two dimensions, the social and the individual. In other words, certain memes, or perceptions, about translation spread, through social interaction, from individual to individual and define the way translation is generally talked about or practised. As an example of 'supermemes', Chesterman (1997: Chap. 1) quotes ideas such as the 'source-target' distinction, **equivalence** and the **free vs literal translation** opposition. Other examples of memes are the **norms** that govern translator behaviour in a given society or more restricted community.

Minimax principle

Also referred to as 'minimax strategy', this is a notion proposed by Jiří Levý to indicate that in the decision-making process of translation the translator, when faced with a problem, tends to resolve for 'that one of the possible solutions which promises a maximum of effect with a minimum of effort' (Levý 1967: 1179) – the effect being measured against the assumed expectations of TL readers.

Misinterpretation

The term refers to a **translation error** resulting from the misunderstanding of the sense or the cultural reference associated with an ST element. Examples include (cf. Delisle et al. 1999: 159): translating the French *il faut substituer un édulcorant au sucre* into *you should substitute sugar for a sweetener* instead of the correct *you should replace sugar with a sweetener*, or translating the German *Männermode-Designer* with *male fashion designer* instead of the correct *men's fashion designer*.

Modulation

This term indicates a **translation technique** involving a change in point in the transfer from SL to TL. Examples concerning French and English would include the following:

ST: *objets trouvés* ('found objects')   TT: *lost property*
ST: *il est facile de démontrer*   TT: *it is not difficult*
     ('it is easy to show').   *to show.*

In Vinay and Darbelnet ([1958] 1995) modulation is seen as involving a wide variety of changes. It can involve negation (as in the second example above) or other types of changes such as a transfer from abstract to concrete meaning (French: *jusqu'à une heure avancée de la nuit* ['until an advanced hour of the night'] / English: *until the small hours of the morning*) or from part to whole (English: *to wash one's hair* / French: *se laver la tête* ['to wash one's head']).

Multimodality

The term refers to the transmission (and reception) of meaning through the composite deployment of different semiotic resources, or 'modes' (see e.g. Taylor 2004). Almost no text is, strictly speaking, mono-modal, as extra-linguistic visual elements (drawings, photographs, graphs) are present in most texts. Hypertexts, films and TV programmes deploy a variety of semiotic modes to a greater extent than printed texts, such that, in them, meaning is always the result of the interrelation between the verbal and the visual. The notion of multimodality is therefore particularly emphasized in research on **audiovisual translation** and **theatre translation**.

Natural translation

This term is sometimes used to indicate translation as carried out 'by bilinguals in everyday circumstances and without special training for it' (Harris 1977: 99). What position does this type of translation have in translation studies? While Harris himself assigned it a central position, other scholars (e.g. Krings 1986) have rejected this view. The tendency today is indeed that of assigning **professional translation** (in a wide variety of fields) primacy as an object of study, although room is sometimes made for the study of translation as performed or discussed by individuals who would not, strictly speaking, fall within the category of professionals (think, for one, of newspaper reviewers who assess translations).

Non-binary error, see **error**.
Non-essentialism, see **essentialism**.

Normalization

Also called 'conventionalization', normalization is the hypothesis that translated texts universally tend to make use of the typical features of the TL to a greater degree than comparable non-translated texts. Translations, in other words, would appear more standardized than texts written in the TL, in that they use certain lexical items with higher frequency, tend to replace dialect in the SL with standard language in the TL, prefer unmarked grammatical constructs and tend to normalize other aspects such as punctuation. Although a few studies have given support to this hypothesis, normalization is seen by some scholars as a controversial notion. As pointed out in Mauranen (2007: 41), when normalization is discussed, it is not always clear whether it is treated as an S-universal or a T-universal (see **universals of translation**). Also, translation is frequently described as language usage characterized by untypical constructs (e.g. in terms of **collocation**), which runs counter the idea of translations as normalized texts.

Norms

Translation norms are identified by studying regularities in the behaviour of translators, in the product of such behaviour, i.e. translated texts, and in the way translated texts are received. More specifically, a norm is a social notion of correctness or appropriateness, one that states (or expects) what acceptable translations should look like, thus influencing the decisions taken by translators. The translation norms prevailing in a given period or community influence all aspects of the translation process. In the preliminary stages of the process, some norms will affect the decision whether to translate a given text or not. Once translation is started, other norms will regulate the kind of global strategy the translators will employ, so that, say, adherence to the source text may be preferred to adherence to the target culture. At a micro-contextual level, complementing linguistic norms, translation norms will affect decisions regarding the adoption of a certain style or of given text-production conventions. The notion of translation norms is central in the target-culture oriented approach to translation that emerged in the 1970s and 1980s, largely in relation to the work carried out by the Israeli scholars Itamar Even-Zohar and Gideon Toury (see **descriptive translation studies**).

The term 'norm' is not to be intended in a prescriptive sense but rather as a category for the descriptive analysis of translation phenomena (Toury 1995: 57). Norms are *not* permanent laws either – they are socio-cultural constraints affecting the process of translation as carried out by the translators who are active in a given culture, community or group. In particular, norms have a 'graded and relative nature' (Toury 1999: 21); they are generally middle of the way between rules (objective norms) and idiosyncrasies (subjective norms) and can be seen as internalized behavioural constraints that embody the values shared by a community regarding what is right and wrong or adequate and inadequate. Functioning as models of behaviour, norms regulate expectations regarding what is appropriate in a translated text, or even what counts as a translated text. In the process of translation, they complement linguistic norms and govern the decisions taken by the translators. Norms can change over time and can be negotiated across different groups (e.g. translators on the one hand and translation critics on the other).

Toury (1995: 54–65; see also **Gideon Toury** in the 'Key Thinkers' section) distinguishes between three types of norms: the *preliminary* norms are those deciding the overall translation strategy and the choice of text to be translated; the *initial* norm regulates the translator's decision to adhere either to the source text (see **adequacy**) or to the target culture (see **acceptability**); the *operational* norms govern the decisions taken during the act of translating. Chesterman (1993, 1997; see also **Andrew Chesterman** in the 'Key Thinkers' section) differentiates between *expectancy* and *professional* norms. The former operate at the reception end and have to do with the TL readers' expectations of what translations should look like, i.e. they ultimately determine what counts as a translation for a particular community. Professional norms are those that govern the methods and strategies employed in the translation process at a professional level.

Describing translation as norm-governed behaviour in a specific social, cultural and historical situation raises a number of issues such as (cf. Schäffner 1999): how do norms emerge in text (and how can they be reconstructed from translated texts)? How do translators acquire norms? Are translators conscious of the norms constraining their behaviour? Who introduces changes in dominant translation norms? Are translators themselves powerful enough to introduce new norms and change existing norms? In order to answer such questions, an appropriate methodology must be established so that norms can be reconstructed from textual features and a detailed description of the society and culture in which norms obtain is needed. For some scholars, considering aspects such as **agency** or *habitus* can help to establish a link between the social plane at which norms operate and the individual intentionality of translators, so as to better investigate the various degrees of choice associated with translation practice in different scenarios.

See also: **laws of translation, universals of translation**.

Overt error

This is a type of error characterized in relation to the strategy of **overt translation** as identified by House (1977, 1997). An overt error results either from a mismatch of the denotative meanings of an ST element and the corresponding TT element or from a breach of the TL system. More specifically, mismatches in denotative meaning can be subdivided into omissions, additions and wrong selections of TL items. Breaches of the TL system, on the other hand, can be subdivided in cases of ungrammaticality (i.e. breaches at the level of the language system) and cases of dubious acceptability (i.e. breaches at the level of usage).

See: **covert error, error**.

Overt translation

This term refers to one of the two major translation types or strategies identified by House (1977, 1997), the other being **covert translation**. An overt translation is one that presents the text explicitly as a translation. The source text leading to such a translation may be of two types (House 1997: 66–69): a text closely associated with a historical occasion (e.g. a speech delivered by a prominent political figure) or a 'timeless' (House 1997: 66) text, i.e. essentially a text of literary status, one that, while, transmitting a message of general significance is also clearly source-culture specific. With these types of texts, a direct match of the original ST function is not possible and the task of the translator is, for House, that of ensuring that the TL reader has access to the cultural and contextual 'discourse world' of the original. In the TT, in other words, the translator aims at matching a 'second level function' (House 1997: 67; see also **Juliane House** in the 'Key Thinkers' section).

Parallel corpus

This term indicates a corpus containing texts and their translations into one or more languages. A parallel corpus can be unidirectional (i.e. containing texts translated from a language A into language B), bidirectional (i.e. with texts translated from language A into B and texts translated from B into A) or multidirectional (i.e. containing translations of the same texts in more than one other language). Parallel corpora can be used for both research and practical purposes. Specialized parallel corpora, in particular, are constructed for domain-specific translation research, for application purposes (e.g. in **machine translation**) or to be used as reference tools (especially in teaching environments – practising translators are warier of corpora although many of them today use **translation memory** systems, which are essentially a tool for constructing and searching corpora of translated texts). For a parallel corpus to be maximally useful, for either research or practical purposes, the texts contained in it should be aligned, i.e. they should be stored in such a way that a given ST element (e.g. a sentence or a paragraph) can be retrieved together with its correspondents in the other language(s). Note, however, that not all text types easily lend themselves to alignment and that, especially in relation to certain language pairs, translation may often entail the relocation of textual segments (typically, phrases or clauses), thus getting in the way of a neat alignment of the texts. This can be particularly problematic when the translations are to be used as reference materials (as in translation memories).

See also: **comparable corpus, corpora**.

Parallel text

The term is used to indicate a text of the same type or on the same topic as the source text, but written in the TL and used by the translator as a source of information. Typically, translators use parallel texts to check actual usage (of terms, phrases and collocations), to learn more about the particular style or rhetorical conventions used in a given text type, or for assistance in comprehending the subject matter treated in the ST they are translating. The term is not to be confused with **parallel corpus**, indicating an electronic collection of translations stored together with their respective STs.

Patronage

The notion of patronage is used by Lefevere (1992: 15) to characterize 'the powers (persons, institutions) that can further or hinder the reading, writing and rewriting of literature' – with power intended not as a repressive force but in the Foucauldian sense of a force that produces knowledge and discourses. Translation is considered by Lefevere as one particular form of **rewriting**. Like other forms of rewriting, it is constrained by the control exerted by patronage, in the sense that translators (like other writers or 'rewriters') accept the parameters set by patrons and choose strategies of translation that are likely to fit or promote such parameters. One particular component of patronage that acts as a constraint on translation is the **ideology** prevalent at a certain time and in a certain culture. By way of example, Lefevere (1992: Chap. 4) examines a number of translations of Aristophanes' *Lysistrata*, focusing on ST passages containing explicit sexual references. The analysis shows how in translation these passages were in many cases suppressed or modified to the point of unrecognizability with respect to the ST.

See also: **poetics**.

Poetics

Poetics is presented by André Lefevere's (1992) as one of the constraints acting on the translation of literary texts. Lefevere (1992: 26) sees poetics as consisting of two components: on the one hand, it is 'an inventory of literary devices, genres, motifs, prototypical characters and situations, and symbols'; on the other, it refers to the particular concept held at a certain time and in a certain society of 'what the role of literature is, or should be, in the social system as a whole'. As such, poetics is seen by Lefevere, in combination with **ideology**, as a constraint that overrides linguistic considerations at every level of the translation process.

Polysystem Theory

Developed by Itamar Even-Zohar in the 1970s, Polysystem Theory provides an account of the way literature in general and translated literature in particular evolve within the larger social and historical framework of a given culture. Literary works are seen as belonging to systems (i.e. groupings or genres such as the literary canon, children's literature or thrillers), with translated literature operating as one such system. Together, these systems constitute the 'polysystem', an inter-related, hierarchical set which undergoes a constant, dynamic process of evolution. The primary positions within the polysystem may be alternatively occupied by more innovative or conservative literary types. Translated literature interacts with other literary types and the way texts are translated is affected by this interaction.

Polysystem Theory emerged as a contestation of established literary canons. Even-Zohar argued that these should include the so-called 'low' literary forms (i.e. non-canonical, peripheral forms such as children's literature and popular fiction) as well as the 'high' forms. As regards translated literature in particular, its potential in initiating innovation and change within a given literary system had hitherto been ignored and one of the aims of Polysystem Theory was to define the circumstances in which translated works might assume particular importance. More specifically, Even-Zohar asked how the need for translations changes as a literary system evolves; he hypothesized that newly evolving literatures translate more texts, while well-established literary systems are less open to external influences and therefore translate less. The quantity and type of translations are thus determined by the historical situation of both the source and receiving culture and the importance of a literary work may be diminished or augmented as, through translation, it enters a different literary system. Usually occupying a peripheral position, translations can assume more prominent roles in literatures that are in the process of being established or are peripheral or are going through a period of crisis. In such circumstances, translated works will be seen to be of primary importance and capable of injecting new life by promoting innovative forms of writing or serving as sources of inspiration.

The position of translated literature within the polysystem is important in that it conditions the operational choices made by translators
(Even-Zohar 1978), who respond to the **norms** and models of the target system. Where translated texts occupy a peripheral position in the
canon, then translators tend to follow existing TL models, emphasizing
the **acceptability** of their choices and remaining closer to target norms.
When translated literature is closer to the centre of the polysystem,
translators tend to favour the **adequacy** of their choices, opting for
solutions that more often break the conventions of the TL and remain
closer to source norms (at the linguistic, textual or aesthetic level).

Postcolonial approaches

Postcolonial approaches to translation can be seen to pursue three
essential lines of inquiry: (1) they study how translation is practised
in cultures emerging from colonialism (see e.g. Tymoczko 1999a);
(2) they look at how the works of writers coming from former colonies are translated into other languages, especially those of the
former colonizers (e.g. Niranjana 1992); and (3) they examine, in
historical terms, the role played by translation in the process of col-
onization (e.g. Rafael 1993) and in establishing the identity of colo-
nized peoples (Cronin 1996). These approaches thus show a wide
variety of interests and themes, but their common, underlying preoccupation is the exposure of the 'hegemonic' structures involved
in translating, or in other words, the ways in which translation is
affected when it takes place between a dominant and a dominated
culture (for an overview, see Robinson 1997a).

Studying French-Arabic translation, with particular reference to
Egypt, Jacquemond (1992) has observed how translators from a hegemonic culture into a dominated one ultimately serve the hegemonic
culture in its desire to integrate its cultural products into the dominated culture. In particular, he notices that: many more texts are translated from a hegemonic culture into a dominated culture than the
other way round; texts translated from a dominated culture into a
hegemonic culture are usually perceived or presented by the receiving

culture as difficult and inscrutable; hegemonic cultures tend to translate works by authors from a dominated culture who conform to the
stereotypes that a dominant culture has of the latter; finally, authors
from a dominated culture who write for recognition (i.e. translation)
by the hegemonic culture tend to conform to stereotypes as perceived
by the dominant culture.

This kind of analysis shows how translation is sometimes constrained by factors mainly having to do with the *source* culture, which
can be seen as running counter the idea that translation is primarily a
fact of the target culture, as maintained by **descriptive translation
studies**. On the other hand, some notions developed by descriptive
studies (e.g. **norms**) have been seen as beneficial in the analysis of
postcolonial writing, i.e. the work of writers coming from former colonies and writing in the language of the former colonizers. Tymoczko
(1999b) sees interlingual literary translation and postcolonial writing
as converging in many respects, as both are concerned with the transmission of elements from one culture to another across a linguistic
and cultural gap. Similar constraints, therefore, can be seen in both
types of writing as regards the representation of material culture
(foods or garments) and social structure, or in the transposition of
proper names (which can be borrowed, translated using established
TL equivalents or accompanied by short explanations). Both types of
intercultural writing can ultimately be seen as oscillating between
bringing the text to the audience and bringing the audience to the text
and both involve norms: preliminary norms (i.e. principles of allegiance
to source or target cultures) and operational norms (i.e. those guiding
micro-contextual choices at linguistic and cultural level). Finally, both
types of writing are subject to parameters determined by **patronage**,
as exercised, for example, by publishers.

Post-editing

The term indicates the editing performed on a text translated by
a **machine translation** system. Post-editing corrects errors and
changes the text for better linguistic quality but in principle it should

preserve as much of the machine output as possible, so that using MT remains economically viable. The level of post-editing ultimately depends on the final use of the translated text. Rapid post-editing may be appropriate for translations having an essentially informative purpose, whereas texts destined for publication may require considerable post-editing to reach publication quality. Post-editing for publication, however, is worth the effort only when MT output is good, so that the text is not to be retranslated from scratch.

See also: **pre-editing**.

Poststructuralist approaches

Poststructuralism is a philosophical current that sees language as indeterminate and incontrollable, a source of potential meanings that ultimately lead to the constitutive instability of the signifying process. Meaning, in other words, is seen by poststructuralists as relational, i.e. not inherent in linguistic symbols, and differential, i.e. not univocal. This view of language is associated with the particular branch of poststructuralism known as *deconstruction,* developed by the French philosopher Jacques Derrida. Derrida himself has written about translation in an essay called 'Des tours de Babel' published in Graham (1985), and the mid-1980s can be seen as the period in which a poststructuralist influence on the study of literary translation began to emerge.

In the deconstructionist view, the meaning of a given word only refers to another word, and this in turn leads to yet another word, starting an indefinite chain of signification that never arrives at a core or centre. It is in this sense that meaning is relational and that words, and texts, have no univocal, pre-assigned meaning. In particular, no text is an original as, by the mechanism of intertextuality or 'iterability', all texts can be seen to recycle and rewrite linguistic forms available from other texts. In the case of translation, if the so-called original text is itself made up of signs that are reused from other texts, then the translation cannot be seen to be subordinated to the original. Instead, the translation acts as a kind of supplement to the text to be translated, its necessary completion as a text lying in wait of further signification. However, because meaning is constitutively elusive and unstable due to the chain of indefinite deferral entered into by signs and texts, translation is also impossible. This dual character of necessity and impossibility can thus be seen as the 'double bind' characterizing any text with respect to translation.

Power

As part of the study of the various constraints acting on translation at social and cultural level, some scholars have devoted their attention to the issue of how power influences decision-making at different levels of the translation process: from the choice of texts to be translated through to the strategies adopted by translators and the ways in which translated works are received in a given culture. Power can thus be defined as the ideological or political stance of those who, in various capacities, exercise control over the steps of the translation 'chain' undergone by texts, thereby including the decision over what texts should be translated (Fawcett 1995; Schäffner 2007). Focusing on power implies looking at imbalances existing between different groups or communities (e.g. translators as against publishers; see Venuti [1995] 2008) or between different cultures.

Questions of power have been looked at primarily in relation to literary translation. Lefevere's (1992) notion of **patronage**, for instance, emerges from an investigation of the role of (economic) power and (political) ideology behind the production of translations. Other questions examined by scholars include translation policies and censorship. Sturge (2004), for example, investigates policies of translation in Nazi Germany, while Rundle (2000) looks at censorship on translations in Fascist Italy. More recently, however, other scenarios of translation besides literature are being considered in terms of the power plays to be observed in them: these scenarios include national and international institutions and more generally all contexts in which political factors can be seen to play a decisive role (for an overview, see Schäffner 2007).

Power differentials between cultures have been discussed particularly in **postcolonial approaches**, which have looked at how translation is affected when it takes place between a 'hegemonic', or dominant, culture and a 'dominated' culture (or former colonizers and former colonies). Another area where the role of power differentials has been analysed is that of **gender**. In particular, feminist theories of translation have looked at the patriarchal ideologies that underpin Western translation theory and at the power structures that derive from them (see e.g. Chamberlain 1988).

See also: **ideology**.

Pragmatic texts

The term is often used to indicate texts that are essentially aimed at conveying information and pay only secondary or no attention at all to aesthetic aspects. They can thus be distinguished from literary or fictional texts.

Pragmatics

Pragmatics is the area of language study concerned with how language is used in communication, and in particular with the way meaning is conveyed and manipulated by the participants in a communicative situation. Pragmatics studies how the interpretation of utterances depends on knowledge of the world, how speakers use and understand **speech acts** and how the structure of utterances is influenced by the relations between participants in the communication. Pragmatics can thus be seen to deal with 'speaker meaning' and the way it is interpreted by hearers (see **implicature**). In translation it can be seen as one of the levels at which equivalence between a ST and a TT can be established. At a more general level, questions of pragmatic meaning can be seen to be of immediate relevance to translation in that they concern aspects such as the intentionality of meaning, the way this is conventionally expressed in different languages, the expectations of hearers/readers and the interaction between utterances and knowledge of the

world – all aspects that are likely to play an important role in the decisions made by translators at the moment of providing a TL rendering
(see Gutt [1991] 2000; Hatim and Mason 1990, 1997; Hickey 1998).
See also: **relevance theory**.

Pre-editing

The term refers to the process of preparing a text for **machine translation**, restricting the range of vocabulary, eliminating potentially
ambiguous passages and changing grammatical structures likely to
represent a source of difficulty for the MT system. Pre-editing may
entail writing a text in *controlled language*, i.e. a carefully constructed
variety of language using restricted vocabulary and simple sentence
structures. The use of controlled language may reduce the burden of
post-editing.

Process of translation

The notion of process essentially serves to distinguish between
translation as a text (or 'product') and translation as an activity.
When seen as an activity, translation can be observed to reflect two
different categories of processes: on the one hand, the cognitive,
psycholinguistic and organizational processes related to an individual translation task, i.e. the mental activity and the behaviour of
the translator carrying out the task; on the other, the social and
physical processes in which various people (not only translators but
also clients, publishers and so on) engage in order to produce a
translation. Studies of translation as process generally adopt one of
two very general perspectives related to the categories described
above. An 'internal' perspective is that adopted by the inquiries into
the cognitive or psycholinguistic processes involved in translation
(see **process-oriented research**). An 'external' perspective characterizes the studies devoted to the relational and social aspects
of translation and the social role(s) played by translators. Studies of
this kind address questions such as the different meanings given to

the notion of translation by different communities (e.g. the general public vs practitioners), the self-image of professional translators or the **norms** adhered to by a given community of translators. The two perspectives, however, must not be seen as mutually exclusive. In areas of inquiry such as translation **competence** the methodology of research can be seen to alternate or integrate 'external' and 'internal' approaches: whether the focus is on the acquisition or the components of translation competence, research in this particular area is confronted with the elucidation of a diverse set of mental and relational processes and skills.

Process-oriented research

The term indicates the research concerned with aspects related to the cognitive, psycholinguistic and organizational processes involved in translation, i.e. the mental activity and the behaviour of a translator carrying out a given translation task (such research is at times also referred to as *protocol research*). Studies in this line of research try to characterize the behaviour and process of translation observed in professional translators (as opposed to other bilinguals or translation trainees), to identify the size of translation units or to describe how trainees develop translation **competence** (in which case the studies tend to be 'longitudinal', i.e. they are carried out over a certain period of time so as to observe how the participants change in relation to the aspect considered). To investigate such aspects, the studies employ empirical data coming from a variety of sources such as the translators' own introspection (see **verbal reporting**), the writing process (see **keystroke logging**), the searches performed by translators in dictionaries or in on-line environments and the focus of attention of the translators as revealed by eye-tracking devices. More recently, data collection methods from the neurosciences have also been used (e.g. electroencephalograms and imaging technologies) so as to gain insight into the neurophysiological processes in the brain which take place while an individual is translating.

Process-oriented research had already been identified by James S. Holmes in 1972 (see Holmes 1988) as one of the branches of descriptive translation studies, but it is customary to mark the beginning of the process-oriented research tradition in translation studies with the publication, in 1986, of H. P. Krings' pioneering work *Was in den Köpfen von Übersetzern vorgeht*, a study investigating the use of time and reference books on the part of translators (Krings' subjects were really language learners) and analysing the nature of both the problems translators encountered and the problem-solving strategies they employed. Krings' study was based on data gathered through verbal reporting, a method originally developed in cognitive science and human information processing. Most of the subsequent process-oriented research in translation has made use of this method, adopting one (or sometimes more) of its possible variants. More recent studies have complemented verbal reports with other data elicitation methods in an attempt to redress what some researchers thought were the limitations of verbal reporting (see **triangulation**).

See also: **product-oriented research**.

Product-oriented research

Research into translation as product, i.e. into translated texts, is generally based on **corpora** of translations (either parallel or comparable) and aims either at establishing whether translated language exhibits features that set it apart from non-translated language (the so-called **universals of translation**) or at identifying regular linguistic patterns that can help to shed light on the strategies and techniques employed by translators in given language pairs, genres or text types. In a wider sense, the term product-oriented research encompasses any study of translated texts. Product-oriented research on translation is generally seen as distinct from **process-oriented research**. However, this identification of two separate strands of research should not be seen as pointing to two completely different and separate areas of investigation each having its specific object. The distinction between product and process should not 'ignore the fact that the one is the result of the other, and that the nature of the product cannot be understood without a comprehension of the nature of the process' (Holmes

1988: 81). The distinction between these two dimensions (product and process) has, in some cases, more to do with the methodological choices made by researchers than with the object of their research. So, for instance, a study such as Campbell (1998), although based on 'products' (more specifically, several translations of the same ST, each produced by a different translator), is aimed at shedding some light on some cognitive aspects of translation, i.e. on 'process'. By the same token, corpus-based studies of translation may lead to an identification of the (process) strategies employed by translators. Corpora, for instance, have been used to investigate the claim that **explicitation** is an inherent feature of translated texts.

Professional translation

A professional translator can be defined as someone who carries out remunerated translation work on a more or less stable basis. Acknowledging the difficulty to define translation as a true profession in the same way as medicine or law are, Chesterman (2001: 146) proposes to consider as a professional translator someone 'who is a translator' as opposed to someone 'who does translations (sometimes)'. It is a fact, however, that translation as a field of economic activity has in the last 50 years acquired traits that are comparable to those found in other such fields, at least in some countries: it is seen to require a certain set of technical skills, it is increasingly institutionalized, it increasingly adopts quality control systems and it relies on accreditation procedures (although these, in particular, are rarely binding). The elaboration of specific training curricula, often offered at university level, is another sign of professionalization, although specific educational qualifications are rarely a requirement with a view to recruitment. Professional organizations have been founded in many countries to represent translators (e.g. the Institute of Translation and Interpreting in the UK, the American Translators Association, the Société Française des Traducteurs and the Bundesverband der Dolmetscher und Übersetzer e. V. in Germany).

Professional translation is today practised as a freelancing activity, in international organizations and in translation agencies, or 'language service providers' as they are sometimes called. Recruitment in the translation departments of companies (especially large multinationals) is not as common as it was in previous decades. Of these different contexts, international organizations such as the EU or the UN are the only ones where translation can be seen to have a structured career path and where an established recruitment policy is in place.

Considerable changes to the scenario of professional translation have been introduced over the 1990s as translation services were geared to industrial processes. These changes are attributable to several factors that can be schematically summed up as follows (Gouadec 2007; see also Sager 1994):

- development of specialized computer aids (see **translation tools**);
- an increase in the amount of material to be translated;
- the increased adoption of standardized procedures in terms of work organization, processes and methods: translation work is today often organized along project lines, with 'project managers' coordinating the workflow and assigning jobs to team members;
- increased adoption of standardized product requirements (i.e. required terminologies and styles as laid out in 'style guides');
- an increase in the number of translation companies (known as *language vendors* in the **localization** industry);
- mergers of companies or acquisitions of translation and language engineering companies by non-translator investors;
- search for productivity gains;
- division of labour and increased specialization;
- introduction of **quality assessment** and **quality assurance**;
- outsourcing (and the consequent elimination of translation departments in companies);
- **globalization**: through computer networks translators can work from anywhere in the world, often participating in 'virtual' teams.

In research on translation, the specific economic aspects of the profession have up to now largely remained in the background and very few studies have looked at how they affect the *linguistic* make-up of translated texts (Mossop 2006: 2). The figure of the 'commissioner', i.e. the individual or entity that initiates a translation task, has often been considered, but always in abstract terms: in **cultural studies approaches** the commissioner is depicted as someone who chooses texts for translation on cultural grounds and imposes an ideological agenda on the translator (see also **patronage**); in **functionalist approaches** the commissioner picks up the *skopos* of the translation and gives instructions, but specifically economic aspects are largely overlooked. Yet it would be interesting to see whether economical aspects, in the sense of the prices, profits, incomes and sales associated with translation carried out at professional level, play a role in affecting the way translators translate from a purely linguistic point of view: e.g. whether tight deadlines (aimed at increasing productivity, that is, profits) lead to more literal translations, or translations that are more idiomatic but less accurate, or translations that use default equivalents even when they are not appropriate (Mossop 2006: 2).

Prototype

The notion of prototype as developed by cognitive sciences has frequently emerged in theoretical discussions of translation, especially as far as issues of categorization are concerned. In particular, it has been used in relation to the concept of **translation** itself and as a basis for providing a translation-oriented **text typology**. The notion of prototype emerges from research on how humans form and categorize concepts and how they decide whether something belongs to a particular category. Such research has shown that categorization is not based on objective qualities but depends on, and is determined by, the properties of humans as cognitive subjects. Concepts emerge from the interaction between individuals and their environment, which implies that categorization is not as objective nor as observer-independent as was classically believed.

To answer the question 'what is meant by the term translation?', especially in relation to translation as an object of study and research, the idea has been put forward that translation could be seen as a concept subject to 'prototype effects' (Halverson 1999). Seeing the concept of translation in this light is considered by Halverson an effective way of settling theoretical disputes over what should be considered a translation (as opposed to a non-translation) and whether certain types of activities are more representative of the concept than others. In particular, looking at translation as a prototype concept means that the centre of the concept is seen to be represented by the kinds of texts that most people, in a given culture and period, consider to be translations, while the periphery is occupied by less typical examples (see also Chesterman and Arrojo 2000: 153). Membership to the category of translation, in other words, becomes 'graded', so that each different notion of translation will occupy a position in the overall category which is closer or farther away from the core, and the core itself can be characterized differently according to the perspective adopted. As an example, consider the different attention granted by scholars to **natural translation** as opposed to **professional translation** – Harris (1977) considers it central in the field; Krings (1986) rejects this view.

As far as text typology is concerned, the notion of prototype is used by Snell-Hornby (1988) with the aim of abandoning categorizations based on 'box-like compartments' (30). Her 'prototypology' locates texts along a spectrum or cline with no clear-cut divisions, each text representing the realization of an underlying ideal prototype which occupies a more central or more peripheral position within three broad areas: literary translation, general language translation and special language translation. The texts so identified are then related to the relevant aspects and criteria governing the translation process, and an indication is provided of the linguistic and non-linguistic disciplines that appear to be of greater significance for each text type. Snell-Hornby's prototypology is proposed as one of the foundations of an approach to the study of translation based on interdisciplinarity (see also **Mary Snell-Hornby** in the 'Key Thinkers' section).

See also: **translation types**.

Pseudotranslation

A text that purports to be a translation but later turns out not to be such, as it has no ST (Toury 1995: 40–52). Such texts may be studied in terms of the socio-cultural situation in which they are produced and of the way they are received by their audience. This can help to shed some light on the features and functions that a given culture associates with translated texts. A 'pseudo-original' is, instead, a text that purports to be an original but then turns out to be a translation.

Quality

The notion of quality concerns, in essence, how good or bad a translation is. As the evaluative judgement implied by this question can be applied to different aspects of a translation, quality is bound to be a relative notion. In other words, it depends on the specific needs, motivations and presuppositions of whoever is responsible for the **assessment** of a translated text. Sager's (1983: 21) remark that there are 'no absolute standards in translation quality but only more or less appropriate translations for the purpose for which they are intended' can now be seen as commonplace in translation research (see also Schäffner 1998).

More specifically, views on quality vary depending on whether translation is seen as a product, a process or a service. The various approaches to quality proposed in translation studies or adopted in the field of professional translation are based on one or the other view. At an academic level, the focus has traditionally been placed on translation as product, i.e. on translated texts, so that quality was assessed primarily in relation to the degree of **equivalence** between TT and ST. Criteria of assessment have then been extended so as to take into account the wide variety of factors that constrain translators' choices in the **process of translation**, from the function of texts (Reiss 1971; House 1977, 1997) through to the expectations of TT readers and the **norms** that govern the activity of translators (Chesterman 1997).

At an industrial level, quality standards for translation are mostly process related: they lay down procedural guidelines and attempt at ensuring customer satisfaction (see **quality assurance**). In general, therefore, the various standards existing for the translation industry do not establish criteria for measuring quality in the translated texts but, rather, look at the correctness and reliability of the procedures adopted to arrive at texts. The assumption is that if there is a system of accountable and transparent quality control for the translation process, the product will turn out to be qualitatively acceptable (which, in turn, implies that all parties involved agree on what an ideal translation is like; cf. Chesterman and Wagner 2002: 81).

The concept of quality is problematic especially where one is not aware of or does not take into account 'the ideas and ideals about translation quality the translator, reviewer, or researcher entertains' (House 1997: 119). The list could be expanded to include clients, i.e. those who pay for a translation job, as they are often likely to have a very different idea of quality as compared to the way it is often presented at academic level or even in training institutions. For example, if clients start from the assumption that translation is primarily a 'service', rather than just a textual product, their idea of quality may easily make room for process-related considerations: a good translation, therefore, is also (and, at times, exclusively) one that is delivered *on time* and in line with the *specifications* provided for the job – the latter covering not only style and terminology but also aspects such as layout or formatting.

Quality assessment

In the context of professional translation, and especially in relation to the translation production chain, this term is sometimes used to refer to the identification (but not the correction) of problems in randomly selected passages of a text 'in order to determine the degree to which it meets professional standards and the standards of the translation organization' (Mossop 2001: 92). The purposes of quality assessment include the evaluation of translator performance or the selection of freelancers.

See also: **quality assurance**.

Quality assurance

In relation to the production chain of translated documents, quality assurance is the set of procedures applied throughout the translation process to ensure that the quality requirements of clients are met. In particular, the procedures are aimed at ensuring quality of service, (e.g. in terms of deadlines), quality of presentation (in terms of layout and format) and linguistic quality (cf. Mossop 2001: 92–93).

See also: **quality assessment**.

Rank-bound translation

In Catford (1965) a 'rank' is a unit of linguistic description of a certain length: a morpheme, a word, a group, a clause or a sentence.
A rank-bound translation is one that provides TL equivalents only
for units at the same rank, e.g. only words for words or sentences
for sentences. For example, a word-for word rank-bound translation
of the English sentence *I go to bed every night at ten* into Italian
is *Io vado a letto ogni sera alle dieci*. Translating the sentence into
Spanish with *Yo me acuesto todas las noches a las diez* would instead
be an **unbounded translation**, with a **shift** from the English verb
phrase (*go to bed*) into a single verb (*me acuesto*) in Spanish that
cuts across ranks.

Realia, see **culture-bound terms**.
Recategorization, see **transposition**.

Relevance theory

The term indicates a cognitive approach to translation developed by
Ernst-August Gutt ([1991] 2000) and based on the 'relevance theory
of communication' elaborated by Dan Sperber and Deirdre Wilson
in their book *Relevance: Communication and Cognition*, first published in 1986. Relevance theory sees communication as crucially
depending on inferential processes. In particular, communication is
seen to result from the interplay between the context, or the 'cognitive environment', of an utterance and the processing effort required
to infer meaning from that utterance. The crucial factor that makes
communication succeed is the pursuit of *optimal relevance* on the
part of both the communicator and the recipient. An utterance is
optimally relevant when: (1) it enables recipients to find the intended
meaning without unnecessary effort; and (2) the intended meaning
provides adequate benefits to the recipients, i.e. it either coincides
with the right inferences or helps them to strengthen or eliminate
their previous assumptions. For example, in the following exchange

(cf. Gutt [1991] 2000: 29):

> A: *Could you have a look at my printer – it's not working right.*
> B: *I have got an appointment at three o'clock.*

if A assumes that the printer problem is a serious one and knows that there are only five minutes to three o'clock, then A's inference from B's reply can only be that B will not be able to have a look at the printer. The intended meaning of B's reply can thus be said to have provided maximum 'contextual effect', meaning that, while giving new information, it successfully interacts with A's assumptions and knowledge, i.e. with the context of the utterance. New information that does *not* interact with the context as seen by the recipient provides no 'contextual effects' and ultimately has no meaning at all.

Thus, according to relevance theory, unless the sender of a message knows something about the recipient's expectations, situational context and cognitive experience, the message cannot be formulated in an optimally relevant way. These three factors are seen by Gutt ([1991] 2000) as playing a crucial role in translation as well. Readers of a translation will have different ideas from readers of the ST about what is relevant to them, given that they have different cognitive backgrounds from ST readers. The translator's task is to translate what is relevant, which may lead to occasionally explaining, adding or omitting things in the TT. In particular, the translator should arrive at the intended interpretation of the ST and then propose the solutions that 'interpretively resemble' the ST and are relevant for the TT audience.

See also: **implicature, pragmatics**.

Resistant translation, see **foreignization**.

Revision

In a general sense, the term revision refers to a comparative check carried on the TT and its respective ST in order to identify problems and errors and introduce the necessary corrections or amendments. In the context of professional translation, revision indicates one particular stage in the chain of production of translated documents and can be defined as the process aimed at identifying features of a draft translation that fall short of the required **quality** standards and at introducing the necessary amendments and corrections. Revision parameters can be seen to refer to four categories of problems found in a draft translation (Mossop 2001: 99): (1) problems of meaning transfer, related to the accuracy or completeness of the TT; (2) problems of content, having to do with the presence of factual errors or logical inconsistencies; (3) problems of language and style, regarding aspects such as the smoothness of the text, the correct use of genre conventions or specialist terminology, adherence to stylistic requirements and correctness of grammar, spelling and punctuation; (4) problems of presentation, having to do with the organization and layout of the document. Revision may be carried out by the same translator who has completed the first draft, as is often the case with freelancers working directly for clients, or by a different translator acting as reviser, as happens in larger translation companies or in the translation departments of some institutions, where the role of reviser is usually taken up by senior translators. In large software or web site **localization** projects, revision may include *functional testing*, which is a check aimed at verifying whether in the translation process errors have been made (e.g. in terms of wrong hyperlinks or altered programming code) which lead to the malfunctioning of the translated software application or web site.

Revoicing

The term refers to a variety of language transfer procedures used in **audiovisual translation**, including **voice-over**, lip-synchronized **dubbing**, **audio description** and simultaneous interpreting. In all of these forms, a certain degree of synchronization between TL voicing and on-screen images is felt to be necessary but it is especially in dubbing that synchronization is considered to be of particular importance. Simultaneous interpreting is often used in film festivals to provide a translation for films that, for reasons of budget or time-constraints, could not be translated by either subtitling or dubbing. In such cases interpreters dub the voices of the various characters in a film, at times with the help of a script.

Rewriting

In relation to the production and reception of literature, translation is seen by André Lefevere (1992) as one particular form of 'rewriting' which, together with other forms such as anthologization, historiography, criticism and editing, plays a major role in the manipulation of literature for various ends. Literature is seen by Lefevere as a complex social system controlled by 'professionals' (critics, reviewers, teachers, translators) that, in turn, act under constraints associated with factors operating in the wider social context in which literature fulfils its 'function'. The control exerted by such factors, operating as **patronage** and **ideology** at the wider social level and as **poetics** at individual or professional level, is what ultimately influences the various forms of rewriting. In the particular case of translation, such control factors are seen to 'dictate the basic strategy the translator is going to use' (Lefevere 1992: 42), thus influencing the choices made at discourse and linguistic level.

Rheme, see **theme/rheme**.

Semantic translation

According to Newmark (1981: 22), this is a translation aiming at rendering the exact meaning of the original while taking into account the 'bare syntactic and semantic constraints of the TL'. For example, a semantic translation for the German *Frischer angestrichen!* would be *Recently painted!*, instead of the **communicative translation** *Wet paint!*, which in many contexts would be a more appropriate solution (Newmark 1981: 54). Semantic translation is presented by Newmark as the method to be preferred for texts in which the form is as important as the content, e.g. great speeches, autobiographical and literary works, but also philosophical, scientific and technical texts showing originality of expression (see also **Peter Newmark** in the 'Key Thinkers' section).

Sense-for-sense translation, see **free vs literal translation.**

Shift

A shift is a linguistic deviation from the original text, a change introduced in translation with respect to either the syntactic form or the meaning of the ST. Considering the differences existing between languages (even close ones such as French and Spanish) at the structural level as well as the different cultural background of audiences in any language pair, shifts can be seen as inevitable features of translations. Indeed, given their presence in any translated text, they have traditionally represented a focus of interest for scholars describing problems of formal correspondence and **equivalence** between originals and translations. In other words, among the basic questions translation theory has tried to give an answer to, two prominent interrogatives are: how can shifts occurring in translation be described and why do they occur?

Various descriptions and taxonomies of shifts have thus been proposed, adopting different perspectives and pursuing different aims. This is reflected in the varying, and sometimes confusing, terminology used by scholars. The term 'shift' itself is used in Catford's *A Linguistic*

Theory of Translation (1965). Other scholars have labelled them 'procedures' (Vinay and Darbelnet [1958] 1995), 'methods' or 'techniques', and as such they are often presented in translator training contexts. Others still (e.g. Chesterman 1997) talk about '(local) strategies', thus emphasizing their problem-solving character and their association with the process of translation.

Early taxonomies of shifts tend to be grounded in linguistic theories or comparative descriptions seeking a certain degree of generality. Catford (1965) sees translation as involving the 'replacement' of a certain SL element with the equivalent TL element. He distinguishes between **rank-bound translation** and **unbounded translation**. In rank-bound translation, an equivalent is sought in the TL with reference to one particular rank only, i.e. only at the level of morpheme, word, group clause or sentence, while in unbounded translation equivalences are not tied to a particular rank. An example of a rank-bound translation at word level is the translation of the French sentence *J'ai lassé mes lunettes sur la table* with *I've left my glasses on the table*. Similar cases of close formal correspondence, however, are rare, as even closely related languages exhibit structural inconsistencies which make formal correspondence difficult to establish. Thus, providing a TL equivalent for a given SL element often involves a shift from formal correspondence. Focusing his description mainly on the grammatical and lexical levels, Catford identifies two major types of shifts: **level shifts** and **category shifts**.

A long-established classification that continues to be popular (and one that has set a terminological standard for the labelling of many types of shifts) is that proposed by Vinay and Darbelnet ([1958] 1995) with particular reference to translation between French and English. Vinay and Darbelnet refer to shifts as *translation procedures*, which they subdivide in the two general classes of *direct* (i.e. literal) and *oblique* (i.e. non-literal) procedures. Direct procedures include **borrowing**, **calque** and **literal translation**, while oblique procedures comprise **transposition**, **modulation**, **equivalence** and **adaptation**. Direct procedures are essentially based on literalness; in cases where literalness is not suitable, e.g. because it leads to a different

meaning in the TL or is impossible for structural reasons, oblique procedures should be used. Because they are presented in relation to
isolated elements, Vinay and Darbelnet's procedures are today seen
as 'atomistic and prescriptive' (Snell-Hornby 2006: 24). Especially in
translation teaching, however, they enjoy continued success, in that
they are felt to provide a flexible set of conceptual tools to describe
translating and translated texts at the linguistic level.

Other scholars have looked at shifts focusing on their role in the
process of translation. Chesterman (1997), referring to them with the
general label of 'strategies', sees shifts as changes made on a TL solution that is felt to be problematic or as ways of manipulating the linguistic material of the ST in order to produce an appropriate target text.
He distinguishes between syntactic, semantic and pragmatic changes
and sees them as ultimately motivated by the **norms** adhered to by
the translator, who in the TT may variously prefer to, say, enhance
communicative effectiveness, conform to the expectations of TL readers or give priority to the formal aspects of the ST.

In general, the various description and taxonomies of shifts proposed
so far are probably one of the 'success stories' of translation theory: as
acknowledged by Toury (1995: 85), although they cannot be used to
explain why translations are the way they are, these taxonomies have
nevertheless provided the field with an 'apparatus for describing all types
of relationship which may obtain between target and source items'. To go
back to the two questions mentioned at the beginning ('How can shifts
be described and why do they occur?'), it can be said, with gross approxi-
mation, that while linguistically oriented theories have focussed on the
categorization of shifts and have tended to explain them with recourse
to the way different languages encode meanings, target-oriented and
cultural approaches to translation use shifts as an instrumental notion to
characterize different concepts of translation, which in turn are seen as
motivated by a wide range of socio-cultural factors.

Simplification

The term refers to the hypothesis that translated texts tend to be sim-
plified, linguistically, compared to non-translated texts. This is one of

the so-called **universals of translation**. Features that would testify to the simplification occurring in translated texts include (cf. Laviosa 2002): a narrower range of vocabulary; a lower ratio of lexical to running words; a lower average sentence length. Not all studies have confirmed this hypothesis. Where untypical TL usage (e.g. unusual word combinations) is found in translated texts, this could be interpreted as the opposite of simplification. In studying simplification, care should also be taken in considering the different levels of language involved (cf. Mauranen 2007: 40). For example, where translations are seen to simplify sentence structure by using fewer subordinate clauses, this could also lead to increased complexity in the TL at the textual level, as the TT becomes more fragmented and less coherent.

Skopos theory (*Skopostheorie*)

Within the **functionalist approaches** to translation that emerged in the late 1970s and 1980s, a key role was played by what has come to be known as *Skopostheorie* in German and '*skopos* theory' in English. The theory, developed by **Hans J. Vermeer** (see the 'Key Thinkers' section) with the contribution of Katharina Reiss (Reiss and Vermeer 1984; for accounts in English, see Vermeer 1989, 1996), sees translation as a form of *action*. As all action, it is governed by a certain aim or purpose, labelled *skopos* (Greek for 'purpose' or 'goal'). The *skopos*, in other words, is the overriding factor governing either the choices and decisions made during the translation process or the criteria based on which a translation is assessed. Translating is thus seen as a purposeful activity: it essentially means 'to have a skopos and accordingly transfer a [text] from its source-culture surroundings to target-culture surroundings, which by definition are different from the former' (Vermeer 1996: 39). More specifically, translation is seen by Vermeer (1986: 33) as an 'offer of information', or **Informationsangebot**, in the target language which imitates an offer of information in the source language.

As regards in particular the formal aspects of the ST, these are preserved as far as possible in the TT as long as they conform to the *skopos*. In some cases, the *skopos* may have to do precisely with the preservation of ST form, as happens in some types of **documentary**

translation. Although it has been developed as a reaction to views of translation centred around the notion **equivalence** between the ST and the TT, *skopos* theory does not ultimately reject equivalence – it implies a change of focus such that equivalence between the ST and the TT is seen as hierarchically inferior to the purpose of the translated text. In other words, both in carrying out and in assessing a translation, the ST is always considered in light of the purpose of the translation, and these are linked primarily with target factors.

Elaborating on the notion of *skopos,* Nord (1997) identifies three different components in it: intention, function and effect. 'Intention' is the purpose that the sender wishes to achieve. 'Function' is a property of the translation itself and is assigned to it by the recipient. 'Effect' refers to what happens in the recipient's mind or behaviour upon reading the translation. In ideal cases, the three components coincide.

See also: **translatorial action**.

Source text

The text to be translated, sometimes also called 'foreign text'.

Specialist translation

The term specialist translation (at times also referred to as *LSP translation*, where LSP stands for Language for Special or Specific Purposes) can be defined as the translation of texts dealing with subject-specific knowledge, using specialist terminology, having a particular communicative purpose and addressing a specific audience (cf. Scarpa 2008). The term is normally used as a general label for the translation of documents and texts pertaining to various domains of specialized activity, thereby including not only scientific and technical domains but also other areas such as law, finance, business and marketing. The translation of such texts is normally carried out as part of a production chain, which, at the very least, involves a translator and a client. Consequently, the term specialist translation may be seen to include most translation activities carried out at a professional level (therefore excluding literary translation and translation for the performing arts).

Speech acts

The theory of speech acts is part of **pragmatics** and is intended to account for how language 'does things' besides 'stating things'. It was first elaborated by the philosopher J. L. Austin in the 1930s and then became widely known with the publication of his book *How To Do Things With Words* in 1962. According to the theory, linguistic utterances are often not intended as descriptive, or 'constative', statements but are used as means of performing certain actions. Statements such as 'I bet you sixpence it will rain tomorrow' or 'I give and bequeath my watch to my brother' (as occurring in a will) do not report or describe anything and cannot be discussed as 'true' or 'false'. Rather, they perform the action that they describe – hence Austin's label of 'performatives' for such statements. In particular, in relation to an individual utterance Austin distinguishes three levels of performance. The first level is that of the *locutionary act*, seen as the act of saying something with a certain sense and reference. The second level is that of the *illocutionary act*, and this the level at which a statement can be seen to perform a certain action, such as promising, warning, betting or apologizing. An illocutionary act may be seen to have varying degrees of 'force' attached to it, meaning that it can be taken in different ways, e.g. as a promise rather than a vague intention. Further, the illocutionary act may not necessarily be taken as such by the recipient or, in other words, the recipient may not understand that the utterance is performing the particular action intended by the producer of the act. Finally, the *perlocutionary act* is the actual effect an utterance is seen to produce on recipients, e.g. deterring, persuading, misleading or convincing. Such effect is to be distinguished from the action associated with the illocutionary act as it is not controlled by the producer of the utterance: the perlocutionary act is what a speaker or writer brings about *by* saying something, while the illocutionary act is performed *in* saying something. Speech acts are discussed by Austin at sentence level and mainly in relation to spoken language.

The aspect of speech act theory to have received the most attention in translation research is the illocutionary force of utterances and the way it can be handled (or mishandled) across languages. This has been observed particularly in relation to politeness and the different ways it is realized across languages. House (1998), for instance, describes how German and English adopt different politeness strategies (German tending to be more direct and explicit, and less reliant on routine formulas than English) and then analyses cases in which such differences may have to be reflected in translation as against cases in which politeness strategies may have to be adapted to TL conventions.

See also: **implicature, relevance theory**.

Style

This is a highly contentious term, disliked by many scholars and researchers because of its vagueness yet frequently used in descriptions of linguistic and translational phenomena. Whatever the different connotations and implications of the term, in describing translational phenomena the term style can essentially be taken to indicate a particular use of language serving given rhetorical or communicative functions, and therefore 'motivated' by these functions as regards such aspects as syntactic formulation, lexical choices and textual properties.

Subtitling

Subtitling provides a written version of the dialogue or speech contained in a film or other audiovisual product, usually displayed at the bottom of the screen. This version is either a translation (interlingual subtitling) or a rendering in the same language (intralingual subtitling). Intralingual subtitling is addressed at the deaf or hard-of-hearing or is sometimes used to provide written support to all viewers, for example when speech is in a non-standard dialect.

Interlingual subtitling is together with **dubbing**, the dominant form of translation used for audiovisual products (for an overview, see Díaz Cintas and Remael 2007; see also **audiovisual translation**). The stretches of text (subtitles) displayed on the screen in interlingual subtitling are subject to inevitable constraints in terms of space, synchronization with speech and processing time on the part of readers. In other words, they should not occupy too much screen space, they should relate to what is being said on the screen and they should not prove hard to process. Widely accepted parameters establish that not more than two lines of text can be shown on screen, with each line accommodating a maximum of 35 characters. Given these constraints, subtitles must give priority to the overall communicative intention of utterances, which leads translators to frequently employ strategies such as deleting, condensing and adapting materials contained in the source text.

The heavy textual re-elaboration presupposed by subtitling is sometimes seen as leading to a neutralization of the non-mainstream identities expressed by the linguistic and stylistic diversity of the source text (Díaz Cintas 2005). Another criticism of subtitling is that it affects the overall viewing experience. On the other hand, advocates of subtitling stress that it respects the aesthetics of the original work, while providing a cheaper and faster alternative to dubbing.

Surtitling

In opera performances, surtitling provides a translation of the libretto, displayed on a screen located above the stage.

Target text

The translated text, or the product of translation.

Term bank

The label 'term bank' is used by some authors to indicate a large computerized **termbase** created within a governmental organization, language planning institution or large enterprise, addressed at a broad range of users and frequently made accessible to external users on CD-ROM or through the internet. An example of a term bank is the inter-institutional terminological database of the European Union, also known as IATE (available at http://iate.europa.eu).

Termbase

A termbase, or 'terminological database', is a collection of term entries stored and organized as an electronic database, which is managed using a so-called 'terminology management system'. Term entries are terminological records giving information about the possible linguistic labels for a given concept, in either one or more languages. In traditional dictionaries entries are organized around words (also called *lemmas*), so that for each lemma the various possible meanings are listed (in one or more languages). Termbases organize entries taking meaning as the starting point. In other words, an entry is supposed to give the various possible linguistic labels for a given concept, in the desired languages and according to the desired degree of specificity. For a given concept an entry will typically indicate a main term (selected according to a certain criterion, e.g. frequency in the domain considered) and the other terms that are used to refer to the concept, either in one or in more than one language. Termbases (and **term banks**) are thus usually defined as 'concept-oriented' language resources.

Besides the term themselves and their equivalents in other languages, a term entry is often designed so as to give further information about the concept it refers to, both of a linguistic and a conceptual nature.

For example, an entry could also include the definition of the term/ concept, an indication of the most frequent collocates (or phraseological units) for a given term, an indication of attested sources, an indication of the related terms contained in the termbase and so on. Such information is presented in the different 'fields' constituting the entry. The type and number of fields included in an entry depend on the users of the termbase. Among users (and creators) of termbase are terminologists, translators, technical communicators and librarians. Each of these groups will have specific terminological needs and decide on the information fields to include in term entries accordingly. Given such characteristics, termbases are usually created to collect the terminology related to specialized subject-matter domains.

Termbases are today always stored as computer databases; as such, they can be searched with queries that are not possible with traditional, paper-based dictionaries and therefore provide more flexible search strategies as well as the possibility to filter queries according to particular criteria. A translator, for instance, could look up in his/ her termbase only the TL equivalents used for a given client but not for others. Several commercially available **computer-assisted translation** tools offer components that can specifically be used to create termbases. Note, however, that freelance translators are often reluctant to use a computerized terminology management system to record their terminological research. Rather, they usually compile their own termbases or 'glossaries' (often consisting of no more than term lists in multiple languages) on an ad hoc basis and store them using standard word-processing or spreadsheet applications.

Terminology

The word terminology is used with different meanings. First, terminology is the set of all terms that are used in a given specialized domain. In this sense, it is synonymous with 'vocabulary'. Terminology is also the name of the discipline that studies the behaviour and use of terms in specialized domains of study or activity (see Cabré 2003). In particular, applying both a monolingual and a multilingual perspective, terminology studies the relationship between concepts and terms, the patterns of term formation and the methodology which forms the basis for terminology management, i.e. the applied activity aimed at creating new terms, structuring and standardizing conceptual/terminological fields, and creating terminological resources such as **termbases** and **term banks**.

Terminology management system, see **termbase**.

Tertium comparationis

This is a Latin expression translated literally as 'the third term in a comparison'. It is used to refer to what is assumed to remain invariant in the translation from one language to another. Theories of translation emphasizing the notion of **equivalence** see this aspect as one of their central concerns.

Text typology

The categorization of text types has been a recurrent concern of translation scholars, based on the assumption that identifying text types according to specific criteria can be a useful starting point for translation analysis and **assessment** or for providing guidelines of a procedural nature. A pioneering work in this regard is Reiss (1971), where texts are classified according to the three main **language functions** as identified by Karl Bühler. In particular, Reiss identifies three text types according to the primary function they realize: *informative texts* have the primary aim of conveying content; *expressive texts* are focussed on aesthetic aspects; *operative texts* serve a primarily persuasive function. Reiss sees the linguistic features of texts (at the semantic, lexical, grammatical and stylistic levels) as influenced by their predominant function and believes that translations should reflect such functions and adjust their linguistic profile accordingly. Reiss also identified a fourth text type, that of *audio-medial texts*, in which the verbal content is adapted to the requirements of a given audio-visual medium.

Newmark's (1981, 1988) categorization of text types is based on Roman Jakobson's classification of language functions, which basically adds three more functions (the poetic, the phatic and the metalinguistic) to those identified by Bühler. As in Reiss' typology, the idea is that in any given text there is one predominant function to be reproduced in the translation. Whereas Reiss' intention in applying the notion of function is primarily evaluative and retrospective (at least in her earlier work), Newmark's adaptation of Jakobson's six functions has a more overtly processual nature, i.e. it leads to the elaboration of a list of guidelines aimed at solving the problems more frequently encountered in translating the text types Newmark identifies.

The typology of texts proposed in Snell-Hornby (1988) is based on the notion of **prototype** and is an attempt at abandoning categorizations based on 'box-like compartments' (1988: 30). In Snell-Hornby's prototypology, texts are located along a spectrum or cline with no clear-cut divisions. An individual text represents the realization of an underlying ideal prototype and occupies a more central or more peripheral position within three broad areas: literary translation, general language translation and special language translation. Locating a text along this continuum helps in identifying its function and in relating it to the relevant aspects and criteria governing the translation process.

A text typology is also proposed by Hatim and Mason (1990) on the basis of the interactional and communicative features of texts (for details, see **Basil Hatim and Ian Mason** in the 'Key Thinkers' section). Strategies and problems related to the translation of non-literary text types are discussed in Trosborg (1997).

Theatre translation

Although in the theatre world and among literary scholars there have traditionally been frequent debates over the respective merits of 'faithful' translations and freer, more performable versions, systematic work on the specific aspects of theatre translation and its differences from other forms of literary translation of literary texts only started to appear in the 1980s, in parallel with the emergence of an interdisciplinary approach to translation (cf. Snell-Hornby 2007).

Unlike other literary texts such as novels or poems, drama texts are written to be spoken or, more specifically, to be *performed* on stage. On this basis scholars have set out to identify criteria to be taken into account when providing a translation which is equally to be performed on stage. Aspects to be taken into account in this respect are summarized by Snell-Hornby (1996) as: the nature of theatre dialogue as an artificial language characterized by special forms of **cohesion**, semantic density, rapid changes of theme and special deictic interaction; the multiple perspectives introduced by elements such as paradox, irony, allusion, anachronism and wordplay; the particular role played by rhythm and tempo; the identification of language with actors, of whom it becomes a sort of 'mask'; and, finally, the role of spectators, who are likely to be emotionally involved in the performance. A consideration of these aspects is felt to be crucial in ensuring that the translation of stage dialogue leads to adequate 'speakability' and 'performability' in the TL. Equally important is the attention given to the socio-cultural circumstances of the translated text: in order to 'work' as an independent text, a translated theatre text may have to be more or less adapted to the particular circumstances of the target culture (see Anderman 2005).

As regards the role of translators in theatre productions, Aaltonen (1997) identifies two categories: the first is that of translators who only act as 'mediators': these provide a TL version but remain outside the production team; the second category is that of translators directly involved in the production, often as dramaturges or directors.

See also: **adaptation**.

Theme/rheme

The notions of theme and rheme can be used to describe how texts are organized in terms of 'information flow', i.e. the way a text develops and conveys information by establishing points of orientation, providing new information and creating internal links between its constituents. Linguistic elements are thus considered not as strings of grammatical or lexical items but as segments that, by contributing to **cohesion** at text level, serve a communicative and interactional function.

In a sentence, the 'theme' is the segment that establishes what the sentence is about, while the 'rheme' is the segment of the sentence that says something about the theme. In languages such as English the theme tends to come in initial position in the clause and does not necessarily coincide with the grammatical subject. In the following example:

> *The external borders of the EU have stretched eastwards to include new member states. Thanks to this enlargement, the mixture of history and culture represented by the EU is now even richer.*

the theme in the first sentence (*The external borders of the EU*) is also the subject of the sentence, while the theme of the second sentence (*Thanks to this enlargement*) is, syntactically, a causal adjunct. The organization of sentences into theme and rheme is also referred to as *thematic structure*, and can be distinguished from what linguists call the *information structure* of sentences and clauses. This refers to the way sentences present information that is 'given', i.e. already provided in previous stretches of text, or 'new', i.e. information that was not previously provided in the text. The theme is usually given information, as it refers to something mentioned before in the text, while the 'rheme' tends to convey new information. Deviations from this pattern, however, are common. In narrative texts, for example, temporal adjuncts are frequently used in theme position to mark the timing of events (e.g. *In August 1941, the Japanese attacked Pearl Harbor. One month later . . .*). Also, establishing whether a segment is given or new information can be seen to depend ultimately on context, as the same utterance may be segmented in different ways in response to different questions. A sentence such as *We're climbing Ben Nevis* is all new information if it answers the question *What's happening tomorrow?* If, however, the question was *What are we climbing tomorrow?* the same utterance could be seen as providing given (*We're climbing* . . .) and then new (. . . *Ben Nevis*) information. Baker (1992: Chap. 5), where the previous example is taken from, gives an extensive treatment of both thematic and information structure and their relevance for translation purposes. In particular, Baker reviews the different positions of linguists over the coincidence of thematic and information structures, focusing, in particular, on the Hallidayan view and the approach of the Prague School linguists, also referred to as *functional sentence perspective*. From a contrastive viewpoint, Baker also points out that analyses of thematic structure may prove difficult with languages with freer word order than English or languages, such as Chinese, where clauses are introduced by a 'topic' element preceding the grammatical subject, which results in sentences structured like the following: *Animals, I advocate a conservation policy* (Baker 1992: 141). In any case, the notions of thematic and information structure may be useful descriptive tools in comparing the way source texts and translations organize the flow of information above the levels of lexis and syntax. As an example, consider the two pairs of sentences below (taken from authentic translations discussed in Rogers 2006: 49, 54):

(1) ST (German): *Die letzte bedeutende Abstimmung gewann die Regierung mit einer Mehrheit von nur einer Stimme.*

TT: *The government won the last important vote in parliament with a majority of only one.*

(2) ST (German): *Für die europäischen Finanzmärkte sind aber auch die Präsidentenwahlen in Russland vom kommendem Juni bedeutsam.*

TT: *For the European financial markets the presidential elections in Russia next June are also important.*

In example 1, the translation keeps the same grammatical structure of the ST (with 'the government'/'die Regierung' as subject of the sentence), which, however, results in a change of communicative perspective, as the theme of the TL sentence ('the government') is different from the theme in the ST ('Die letzte bedeutende Abstimmung/the last important vote [in parliament]'). Notice that a passive structure in English might have retained the theme ('*The last important vote in parliament* was won by the government with a majority of only one'). The translator, however, may have opted for a change in thematic progression as a means of improving the flow of information at textual level. In example 2 both sentences have the same theme ('Für die europäischen Finanzmärkte/For the European financial markets') and this is in neither case the subject of the grammatical subject of the sentence (i.e. 'die Präsidentenwahlen in Russland vom kommendem Juni'/'the presidential elections in Russia next week'). In this case the translator has probably felt that the communicative perspective of the ST could be retained with no consequences on the flow of information at textual level.

Theory of Sense, see **interpretive approach**.

Thick translation

This term is used by Appiah (1993) to indicate a translation rich in annotations and glosses aimed at locating the text in its cultural and linguistic context. Appiah uses the term specifically for the translation of proverbs in the Twi language, spoken in Ghana. Thick translation can be seen as a form of ethnographic translation.

Think-Aloud Protocol

In the 'think aloud' method of data collection a translator is asked to translate a text while concurrently verbalizing as much as s/he can of his/her thoughts. The verbalization is audio- or video-recorded and then transcribed: the transcript is referred to as the Think-Aloud Protocol (or TAP) and constitutes the object of study on the part of the researcher, with or without reference to the actual recording.

TAPs and other types of **verbal reporting** are methods of data collection used in **process-oriented research**. They are based on the assumption that human cognition is information processing and that information is stored in memories with different capacities. Researchers have used TAPs to investigate specific questions such as problem-solving strategies (Krings 1986; Lörscher 1991), the use of reference materials (Livbjerg and Mees 2003) and the differences between novices and professionals (Jääskeläinen and Tirkkonen-Condit 1991). After a first, enthusiastic phase (which, in chronological terms, goes from the publication of H. Krings' pioneering study in 1986 till the second half of the 1990s), the use of verbal reporting in process-oriented studies of translation has come under closer scrutiny, as it has been felt that the validity of the method had previously been 'assumed rather than proved' (Bernardini 2001: 242). Some reservations have been put forward as regards particularly the use of TAPs with professional translators: as some of their skills have been automatized, they may by-pass Short-Term Memory and may therefore not be available for verbalization. Other concerns voiced by researchers (see Tirkkonen-Condit and Jääskeläinen 2000) have had to do with the potential effect of verbalization on the process being investigated, the lack of a clear definition of the object of study in many TAP-based investigations, and the lack of a clear definition of the notion of 'problem' in those studies which had this notion as their object, either implicitly or explicitly. More recently, studies using TAPs have combined them with other methods of data collection so as to test hypotheses on firmer empirical ground (see **triangulation**).

Thanks to TAPs and other similar methods a number of aspects related to the translation process have been elucidated. Text processing, for instance, has been shown not to be linear but recursive. Also, some studies have shown that translator behaviour differs according to the 'routineness' of the task and that the aspects influencing the performance of a translator include his/her emotional state and level of involvement in the task. As regards the differences between novices and professionals, it has been observed that the latter are more aware of aspects such as the function of the translation and the expectations of TT readers.

Third code

The term is used in Frawley (1984) to indicate how, from a semiotic perspective, a translation takes over SL and ST features and combines them with those of the TL so as to emerge 'as a code in its own right' (1984: 169) which is derivative of the ST and TL but establishes its own plane of signification.

Transcoding

The term is used to indicate the replacement of SL units (at the level of word, phrase or clause) with equivalent units in the TL. The notion implies that SL units have relatively stable TL equivalents, to be chosen as translations largely irrespective of the TT function or communicative relevance. At the level of words, transcoding can therefore be seen as another label for 'word-for-word' translation. For example, a sign saying *Working* might be transcoded in French as *Qui fonctionne* or in Italian as *Funzionante*. If we imagine the sign on a vending machine, however, a translation into the two languages would probably read *En service* and *In servizio* respectively.

See also: **free vs literal translation**.

Translatability

Translatability can be seen as the capacity of meaning to be transferred from one language to another without undergoing fundamental change. Translatability and its negative counterpart, *untranslatability*, have been the object of intense debate in traditional philosophical discussions of translation. Different views on the possibility of translating between languages have been proposed by thinkers over the centuries, resting ultimately on their own particular views on the relation between language and meaning.

For those who see meaning as closely associated with language, translation is fundamentally an impossible task. The roots of such views can be traced (cf. Chesterman 1997: 10–12) in the Biblical legend of the

Tower of Babel, the Aristotelian tendency to describe reality according to discrete categories (thus rejecting the fuzziness often implied by translation) and the presentation of the divine Word as sacred and immutable. These views believe in a close relationship between language and meaning and tend to see **equivalence** between languages as unattainable (see also **poststructuralist approaches**).

Other thinkers see the relationship between language and meaning as entailing looser ties or remark the fundamental indeterminacy common in both translation and most other forms of communication (see **indeterminacy of translation**). These thinkers tend to emphasize the possibility of translation, although often considering restrictions and qualifications of varying degrees and nature, which in turn leads them to conclude that equivalence across languages is bound to be partial and relative. The much-quoted position of the German philosopher Walter Benjamin ([1923] 1963) sees languages as sharing a fundamental affinity that translation helps to unearth.

Hermeneutic approaches take an intermediate position between the two extreme poles of translatability and untranslatability. They emphasize the incommensurability of languages but also the possibility to access meaning through various modes of understanding the foreign text. Whatever philosophical position is assumed, the actual practice of translating (carried out on texts of an immense variety of types and genres) attests to the possibility of translation, although varying degrees of **difficulty** can be seen to be attached to any translation task, depending on factors such as the pair of languages involved, the type of text to be translated and the purpose of the translation.

Translation

A translation may be defined as a text in one language that represents or stands for a text in another language; the term translation also refers to the act of producing such a text. Over the centuries, Western theoretical reflection about translation has centred essentially on its very possibility (see Ballard 1992; Vermeer 1992; Robinson 1997b) and tried to establish whether and to what extent the meaning of a text in one language can be transferred to a text in another language. Views have oscillated between positions that maintained the impossibility of the task and positions that, while acknowledging that a text translated in a given language can never be the same as a text in the original language, nevertheless recognized that translation is possible. Different methods of translation and the respective merits have been proposed, stressing either the need to remain as close as possible to the original text or the necessity of adhering to TL rhetorical or stylistic models. Overall, the traditional debate on **translatability** can be seen as a reaction to early Platonic ideas about the possibility of carrying meaning across languages while leaving it unchanged (cf. Chesterman 1997: 21).

In modern research, starting roughly at the end of World War II, the possibility of translation tends to be taken as a given and reflection at a theoretical level (now configured as a scholarly activity) is primarily concerned with the nature of the relation established between original and translation and the function of translations in the TL context. Linguistic approaches tend to equate translation with an act of decoding and recoding. Catford (1965: 20) defines it as 'the replacement of textual material in one language (SL) by equivalent material in another language' and studies it mainly at the level of words and sentences. Later linguistic approaches take the text as their frame of reference and tend to see translation as re-textualization, or 'source-text induced target-text production' (Neubert 1985: 18). In most linguistic approaches translation involves a relationship of **equivalence** between the ST and the TT. To specify possible types of equivalence, different typologies have been proposed, such as Nida's (1964) and Koller's (1979).

Other modern approaches see translation as a phenomenon characterized by variability and discuss it in more decidedly functional terms. These approaches, in other words, are interested in what translation *does* (mainly in the target culture) rather that in what translation inherently *is*. Toury (1999: 11), in particular, sees such variability of translation as 'difference across cultures, variation within a culture and change over time'. Equivalence and types of equivalence are, in these approaches, not postulated but observed *a posteriori*: a translation is any text that is presented as such.

Approaches to translation based on hermeneutics and poststructuralism tend to see language as constitutive of meaning (rather than expressive of meaning) and characterize translation as a creative reshaping of the ST. Presupposing a fundamental difference between languages, these approaches see translation as a form of understanding and are concerned with the ways in which this understanding can be linguistically expressed in the TL. Such preoccupation is often seen (cf. Berman 1984; Venuti [1995] 2008) to have ethical implications, as the task of the translator is thought to involve the preservation of foreignness. Translation, in other words, should reshape an ST not as a way of affecting naturalness but, on the contrary, as a way of letting its otherness emerge.

The diversity of conceptual approaches in contemporary research on translation has led some scholars (e.g. Halverson 1997) to propose a view of translation as a **prototype** category having more typical examples at the centre and less typical examples at the periphery. Such a view allows the inclusion, within the sphere of translation, of types of texts that have at times led to controversy as regards their characterization as translations (e.g. the texts resulting from **adaptation** or from **natural translation**).

Translation aids

This is the term used in Delisle et al. (1999) to indicate any tool that helps the translator, including dictionaries, reference works and computerized **translation tools**.

Translation brief

The translation brief (or translation commission) is the set of specifications given by a client to the translator in relation to a particular translation job. A brief can give information as to the purpose of the translated text, the client or intended audience, the stylistic guidelines to be followed, the terminology to be preferred and other aspects such as layout and formatting. The notion of translation brief is often used in translation studies to refer to the explicit or implicit specifications for any given translation task. As such it may be used as a parameter in discussing the application of a particular **translation strategy** or in the **assessment** of translated texts.

Translation commission, see **translation brief**.

Translation criticism

The term is sometimes used as a synonym for translation **assessment**. In a narrower sense, it may refer to the reviewing of translated literature as found in newspapers or review journals. Fawcett (2000) has studied the reception of translations in the UK press.

Translation error

A translation error is any fault occurring in a translated text and resulting either from ignorance or from the inadequate application of a **translation technique** or **translation strategy** (cf. Delisle et al. 1999: 189). Broadly speaking, errors in translation may be seen to regard the inaccurate transfer of ST content or the wrong selection of TL alternatives in terms of style, register or other aspects linked to the specifications associated with the translation task. The concept of translation error lies in a much larger field of translation research, which is that of translation **assessment**, and is also linked to at least two other broad areas of research: translation **competence** and translator training. Within translation assessment, the discussion of errors is part of the investigation of assessment criteria and assessment procedures and instruments. From an applicative point of view, the particular context in which assessment takes place has to be taken into account, and in this sense a general distinction can be made between translation teaching and professional translation. The definition of translation error will change according to the particular context where assessment is carried out, although elements of the definition are bound to overlap to a greater or lesser extent.

Traditional typologies of translation errors are based on categories such as **incorrect meaning**, **misinterpretation** and **interference**. These categories have mostly to do with faulty transfer of the sense expressed by the ST, especially at word, phrase or sentence level. Despite criticisms emerging as far back as the 1970s, they are still popular in translator training. Their continuing success is perhaps due to three main factors (Waddington 1999: 37): (1) the sheer force of habit; (2) the fact that they are more or less overtly based on the principles of the *stylistique comparée*, an approach which was very influential in translation research starting from the 1950s (cf. Vinay and Darbelnet [1958] 1995); and (3) their simplicity of use.

Criticisms directed at traditional categories of translation error are mainly concerned with their rigidity and their insistence on translation as having an essentially linguistic, rather than communicative, dimension (cf. Gouadec 1989: 36; Waddington 1999: 64–65). The rigidity derives from their tendency to establish universally valid parameters which do not take into account the uniqueness of each ST, if not of any act of translation. Furthermore, their lack of a communicative perspective makes these categories unable to evaluate a given TT element in terms of its **appropriateness** to the TT function or genre or to any other pragmatic consideration entering the transfer process or explicitly linked to the **translation brief**.

The first explicit attempt at accounting for a functionalist perspective in the evaluation of translation errors is to be found in House (1977, 1997), where a distinction is proposed between **covert error** and **overt error**. The identification of two broad categories of errors, usually with one category including errors identified in terms of the specific translation task at hand and the other concerned with errors resulting from a general lack of linguistic or cultural competence, is to be found in most of the subsequent studies dedicated to either translation errors or translation assessment. Gouadec (1989) makes a distinction between *absolute* and *relative* errors. Absolute errors result from a violation of the cultural or linguistic norms or from a violation of usage rules, while relative errors are solutions that do not conform to the requirements of a given translation project. Other categorizations of errors introduce finer levels of detail, relating errors to various different dimensions of interlinguistic transfer. Nord (1997: 75–78), for instance, makes a distinction between *pragmatic*, *cultural*, *linguistic* and *textual* errors. As a consequence of such distinctions, the **quality** of a translation is seen as relative concept; its measurement is not based on absolute standards but is carried out in terms of appropriateness with respect to the purpose of a translation or to the particular dimension considered. By the same token, the impact of errors is seen as varying according to the relative importance of the erroneous element within the text as a whole (cf. Kussmaul 1995: 139–141).

A popular general categorization of errors is that provided by Pym (1992), where a distinction is made between *binary* and *non-binary* errors. A binary error opposes a wrong TL solution to the right TL solution: examples would be language errors or wrong TL terminology. Non-binarism, on the other hand, 'requires that the target text actually selected be opposed to at least one further target text[2] which could also have been selected, and then to possible wrong answers' (Pym 1992: 282). In other words, non-binary errors are those that provoke in a translation teacher reactions such as 'It's correct, but . . .'. In Pym (1992) translation errors 'proper' are identified with non-binary errors as translation competence is essentially seen by Pym to equate with the ability to select the most appropriate solution from a range of possible TL solutions (see also Pym 2003). This position has later been revised by reference to the notion of *risk*: Pym (2004) sees success in translation as essentially a matter of avoiding TL solutions that do not fulfil the purpose of the translation. Good solutions are those that avoid this risk with little effort on the part of the translator; bad or erroneous solutions are those that run this risk even after the translator has invested a lot of effort in them.

Translation memory

An electronic database containing translated texts stored together with their originals; it is managed by special software tools that allow the instant retrieval of text segments together with their translations. The texts stored in a translation memory are normally segmented into units one sentence long and comprise both source and target text. The purpose of storing texts this way is to reuse past translations when a new SL sentence occurs which is identical or similar to a segment contained in the database, thus facilitating and speeding up the production of new translations. The texts suitable for translation with this type of tool are those with a significant degree of internal repetition (in terms of sentence structure and vocabulary) or texts that are frequently updated and retranslated.

The main function of the software that manages a translation memory is to verify whether a new sentence to be translated matches a sentence already stored in the memory. If a match is found, its translation is proposed to the translator, who is free to accept, modify or reject it (remember that the TL solution so proposed is not the result of automatic translation; it is only retrieved from the database). In particular, the extraction of segments is based on two types of matches: a *perfect* (or *exact*) *match* occurs when the new SL segment is perfectly identical (even down to punctuation) to the one contained in the memory together with its TL equivalent. A *fuzzy match* occurs when the extracted segment (e.g. *Click on the OK button*) is not perfectly identical with but only similar to the segment to be translated (e.g. *Click on the CANCEL button*): the TL segment proposed by the memory will in such cases only act as a loose suggestion to be modified in the relevant parts. Over time, as new texts are translated using a translation memory and feeding it with translated segments, enormous collections of sentences and their corresponding translations are built up, ready to be reused. Another way of enlarging (or creating anew) a translation memory is to automatically align source and target segments from already translated texts and feed them into the memory. Translation memory systems often interact with terminology management systems so as to combine the retrieval of segments with that of individual terms taken from a **termbase**.

Translation problem

Translation is often characterized as a problem-solving activity, with problems seen as items, features or aspects of a given ST that pose some kind of **difficulty** for the translator or require the translator to provide TL solutions that are not retrieved through automatic or routine processes. In other words, a translation problem can be defined as any element or aspect found in the ST or related to the translation task for which the translator does not readily find a TL solution or rendering judged to be adequate on the basis of the translation **norms** s/he is adhering to. Most studies of translation regarding the linguistic or textual levels revolve, implicitly or explicitly, around the notion of translation problem. In particular, both **product-oriented studies** and **process-oriented studies** are often concerned with the identification of the **translation strategy** used to solve a translation problem. In some cases, scholars start from a pre-conceived notion of problem (e.g. the translation of metaphors or that of compound nouns in English) and look at how one or more translators have dealt with it. In other cases, the research may be aimed at establishing what translators themselves see as problematic (based, for instance, on data relating to the **process of translation**) Problem-solving abilities are taken to be at the heart of translation **competence** and problems (and the way they are solved) are also one of the crucial aspects taken into consideration in the **evaluation** of translations.

Given its centrality, it is perhaps not surprising to find that many different definitions have been proposed for the term 'translation problem', although not always explicitly and often in studies devoted to other aspects of translation. Traditionally, problems have been seen as linguistic (lexical, syntactic or stylistic) discrepancies between SL and TL texts (Vinay and Darbelnet 1958; Catford 1965). Later treatments and definitions take more explicitly into account the communicative dimension of translation and the need to evaluate a problematic element in terms of the textual function and the other pragmatic considerations entering the transfer process or explicitly linked to the **translation brief**.

In process-oriented studies of translation problems are seen as those aspects of the SL texts that translators tackle by adopting a certain strategy. Lörscher (1991: 79–81) sees a problem as occurring 'when a subject realizes that, at a given point in time, s/he is unable to transfer or to transfer adequately a source-language text segment into the target language' (1991: 80) – a definition given from the perspective of the subject rather than that of the researcher. Lörscher (1991: 85) also notes that problems do not necessarily surface in the products of translation: 'problems in the reception of the source-language text need not necessarily cause problems in the production of the target-language text'. By the same token, 'subjects could have latent problems in SL text reception which would become manifest if the task was to understand the SL text, but which remain latent in translation and do not cause problems in TL text production either' (Lörscher 1991: 85). From the point of view of translation as process, seeing translation problems as elements for which no TL equivalent is directly or routinely provided implies a dynamic and relative character for the notion of problem, as problematic elements probably differ according to the level of experience or professionalism of translators. In other words, certain aspects of the translation task that constitute problems for novices would probably not be problematic for professionals because they are dealt with through routine processes acquired by experience.

In product-oriented studies, problems have often been seen as the other side of the coin of a much more studied aspect, i.e. **translation error**. There is, furthermore, a tendency in some authors to further distinguish between 'problems' and 'difficulties', although the distinction is not always clear-cut. From an essentially pedagogical viewpoint, Nord (1991, 1997), for instance, sees problems as objectively identified phenomena of a textual, pragmatic, cultural or linguistic nature. Difficulties, on the other hand, are a subjective phenomenon depending on the individual translator (or trainee) and arising because of 'deficient linguistic, cultural or translational competence' or because of a lack of 'appropriate documentation' (Nord 1997: 64).

Acknowledging the centrality of the notion of problem, Toury (2002) shows how the term is really used in translation studies with three different senses, serving three different kinds of expert discourse on translation. The first sense (which Toury refers to as 'PROBLEM₁') is located in discussions of the ST and involves issues of **translatability** rather than actual translation. PROBLEM₁, in other words, is a prospective notion that refers to an SL element (e.g. a metaphor) for which we investigate the possibility of establishing optimal correspondence with an appropriate TL element. This investigation is not linked to any actual translation act; rather, the nature of the translation act is only speculated on in idealized terms and a translator 'persona' is postulated who 'is often ascribed almost mythical qualities: full mastery of the languages and cultures involved in the act, unlimited resources, unlimited memory, an ideal capacity to analyze and interpret texts, and the like' (Toury 2002: 62). The second sense identified by Toury ('PROBLEM$_2$') refers to actual instances of translation: it is associated with individual translation acts situated in a particular time and space. This meaning features eminently in product-oriented studies, or discourses on translation which are retrospective and see translated texts as a reservoir of realized TL solutions. In particular, PROBLEMS$_2$ are 'reconstructed entities' (Toury 2002: 64) arrived at through an examination of pairs constituted by an ST segment and its correspondent TT segment. The third sense ('PROBLEM$_3$') is also associated with a single translation event but, unlike the second, it is not retrospective in nature; rather, it considers the event as it is unfolding. It is in this sense that the notion of translation problem is usually looked at in process-oriented studies, especially where they observe the various alternatives proposed by a translator before arriving at a final TL rendering (e.g. using data obtained through **verbal reporting** or **keystroke logging**).

Translation procedure, see **translation technique**.

Translation strategy

The term strategy is used by scholars to refer either to a general mode of text transfer or to the transfer operation performed on a particular structure, item or idea found in the source text. The formal or theoretical status of the concept varies greatly as do the perspectives adopted in approaching it: some scholars have used the notion of strategy with explicitly prescriptive intentions, offering models for either the production or the assessment of translations; others have looked at translation strategies from a descriptive point of view; others still have resorted to mixed approaches, describing certain modes of text transfer and then discussing their respective merits in accordance to a given socio-cultural programme – as does, for instance, Venuti (1995) with his distinction between **domestication** and **foreignization** as general modes of text transfer.

A broad definition is provided by Jääskeläinen (1993: 116), who sees strategies as 'a set of (loosely formulated) rules or principles which a translator uses to reach the goals determined by the translating situation in the most effective way'. Other definitions (cf. Krings 1986: 175; Lörscher 1991: 76; Chesterman 1997: 92) take a narrower view and relate the notion of strategy to that of 'problem'. A translation strategy thus becomes a procedure or method used to solve a particular kind of problem posed by the text to be translated or linked to the translation task. Different kinds of strategy are used for different kinds of problems (cf. Chesterman and Wagner 2002: 57): *search* strategies are used in order to solve search problems; *creativity* strategies are those resorted to when a 'blockage problem' emerges, i.e. when the translators 'gets stuck' on some element of the ST; finally, *textual* strategies are required for solving textual problems. This last category is the one that has so far received the most attention on the part of scholars and researchers.

Textual strategies 'have to do with how the translator manipulates the linguistic material in order to produce an appropriate target text' (Chesterman 1997: 92) and can be applied at global or local level (cf. also Jääskeläinen 1993: 116). Global strategies are applied in more than one part of a text and amount to a particular approach followed by the translator in consistently solving problems encountered throughout an ST. They can be seen as general modes of text transfer: examples include **adaptation** or the opposing strategies of **overt** and **covert** translation (House 1977, 1997). Local strategies concern shorter textual segments; they have variously been characterized as transfer operations, **shifts** or **translation techniques** and are the subject of many classifications (e.g. in Vinay and Darbelnet [1958] 1995; Nida

1964; Catford 1965; van Leuven-Zwart 1989/1990; Chesterman 1997). As noted by Chesterman (1997: 93) himself, whatever the formal or theoretical status of the notion, strategies 'provide useful conceptual tools for talking about translation, for focusing on particular things that translators seem to do, and for improving translation skills'.

Translation studies

Translation studies is a wide and varied area of enquiry having the study of translating and translations as its core. It emerged as a distinctive field of academic study over the last 50 years and, in the English-speaking world, received its current denomination by the Dutch-based American scholar James S. Holmes, in a paper delivered in 1972 (the paper, however, only gained wide circulation in the 1980s; it is reprinted in Holmes 1988). Before the current denomination, the label 'translation theory' was common. As regards other languages, denominations include *Translationswissenschaft* in German and *traductologie* in French.

Most scholars would today agree that translation studies constitutes a discipline in its own right, but opinions differ as regards both its internal structure and the nature of its connections with neighbouring disciplines such as linguistics, semiotics, comparative literature, cultural studies and anthropology. Venuti (2004: 2–6) sees translation studies as a fragmented 'emerging discipline', having different centres and peripheries and encompassing several sub-specialties; he recognizes, however, that the various approaches adopted by scholars have also been capable of 'productive syntheses'. Others scholars (e.g. Hatim 2001: 8–10), while recognizing the plurality of approaches, the diversity of their aims and objectives and some permanent scepticism on the part of both practising translators and applied linguists, see the discipline as consolidating. Others scholars still (e.g. Snell-Hornby 1988) emphasize the interdisciplinary nature of translation studies. An attempt at a unifying definition is provided in Chesterman (2004a), where translation studies is presented as having as its object of research the *relations* that a given translation (or set of translations) has with factors such as:

- the ST, hence the focus on **contrastive analysis**, types of **equivalence** and the notions of translation **shift** and **translation strategy**;
- other comparable texts in the TL, hence the interest in TL **acceptability** or in discovering distinctive traits of translated language; (the so-called **universals of translation**)
- the conditions of TT production, in terms of the people involved (clients, publishers, informants) and the conditions of work for translators (time available, tools used);
- the TT producers themselves, observed for their psycholinguistic and cognitive processes or from sociological and historical perspectives;
- the readers, considered for their expectations or actual reactions;
- the medium, e.g. written text as opposed to audiovisual text;
- socio-cultural aspects such as the **norms** prevalent in a given community and the relations established via translation between different language communities (to be observed in terms of **power** struggles or ideological conflicts; see **ideology**), all of which can be also considered from a historical perspective.

For Chesterman, in sum, studying translation means investigating how these and other factors act as constraints either on the way translators translate or on the way translations are received.

Another interesting aspect of the emergence of translation studies is its pattern of development in different parts of the world. As acknowledged by Venuti (2007: 294), for instance, translation studies is still 'very much a fledgling discipline' in the United States, at least in comparison with academic trends in Europe and Asia. Scholars in Europe and America, on their part, have recently started to discover traditional 'non-Western' approaches to translation, sometimes using them to reconceptualize (as in Tymoczko 2007) the notion of **translation** itself.

Translation technique

The term usually indicates a strategy adopted for the translation of a specific ST element. Examples of techniques are **modulation**, **transposition** and **explicitation**. Other terms used by scholars to refer to such strategies include 'translation procedure' and 'translation shift'.

See also: **shift, translation strategy**.

Translation tools

This is a label commonly used to refer to the various software applications and systems that support the work of professional translators (see Quah 2006). A restrictive definition would include only such tools as **machine translation** systems, **translation memory** systems and terminology management systems (see **termbase**). Broader definitions might include other types of software applications or computerized systems normally used by all professional translators, e.g. word processors. In relation to the **localization** industry, the definition might be extended to include the tools more specifically related to the operational or management aspects of translation projects.

Whatever the definition and scope considered for the term, it is a fact that today all translation performed at professional level involves the use of computers, if only for word processing. Reference works for translators have also been remarkably transformed by the advent of computers. Traditional printed dictionaries are today usually accompanied by electronic versions (either on CD-ROM or, increasingly, as web sites), often offering new, and more effective, search capabilities. Terminological resources are today mostly available in electronic database format and are sometimes accessible through the internet (see **term bank**). It is often the case, however, that adhoc resources are entirely by-passed and translators seek relevant information on the internet using search engines (a modern way of arriving at what were once called **parallel texts**) – unless of course use of a given terminological resource is required by the client.

Translation types

Typologies of translation can be constructed with reference to different criteria and at different levels of generality. At its most general, such a typology may have the aim of delineating the category of 'translation', identifying subcategories (with varying degrees of specificity) and describing the relations obtaining between these subcategories. A popular typology of a general nature is that proposed by Jakobson (1959), in which translation as a superordinate category is seen to comprise the subcategories of **intralingual, interlingual** and **intersemiotic translation**. Other typologies may not refer to what translation 'is' but, rather, to different modes of translation. The opposition **free vs literal translation** may be seen as a general typology in this respect. Other types identified following the same general criterion are House's (1977, 1997) **overt** and **covert translation**, Newmark's (1981) **semantic** and **communicative translation**, Nord's (1997) **documentary** and **instrumental translation** and Venuti's (1995) **domestication** and **foreignization.** Each of these types referring to a general mode of translation may also be seen to correspond to a particular **translation strategy**, described from the specific perspective of interest adopted by the scholar who has identified it. Besides these general distinctions, other typologies may be based on:

- the person who performs a translation, which can lead to a distinction between **natural** and **professional translation**;
- the type of text to be translated, so that broad distinction can be made between literary and **specialist translation**;
- the medium for the material to be translated (see e.g. **audiovisual translation** and **localization**);
- the particular tools employed to carry out a translation task (see e.g. **computer-assisted translation, machine translation**).

An example of a more detailed typology is provided by Gouadec (1990, quoted in Sager 1994: 184), who, for **pragmatic texts**, identifies seven possible types of translation: keyword translation, i.e. translation of the ST keywords; selective translation, i.e. elimination of all irrelevant information; abstract translation, i.e. a summary of the ST; diagrammatic translation, i.e. one conveying ST content in the form of diagrams; translation with reconstructions, i.e. a translation focusing on content alone; absolute translation, i.e. a translation taking into account all aspects of the ST; and sight translation, i.e. a quick, unpolished reformulation of the ST made for informative purposes. As suggested in Chesterman and Wagner (2002: 50–51), recent typologies of translation have focused more on the criteria for classification than on the definition of types. Such criteria take into account aspects such as the intended function of the translation compared to that of the original, the extent to which content is translated in the TT (as in Gouadec's typology mentioned above), the style of the translation, the relative status of the ST and the TT, the naturalness of the language employed by the translator and so on. The aim in these descriptions is to make generalizations about typical features of a given type of translation.

Translationese

This is a term used, most of the time pejoratively, to refer to the unnatural or awkward style of translated texts, especially as produced by the influence of SL structural features.

Translatorial action (*Translatorisches Handeln*)

This is the label used by the German scholar and translator Justa Holz-Mänttäri (1984) for her theoretical model of translation, which is based on the process of translation as carried out at a professional level. Translation is seen by Holz-Mänttäri as involving a complex of actions in which extralinguistic factors play a crucial, controlling role (hence her rejection, in German, of the word *Übersetzung*, 'translation', felt to be too strongly associated with language transfer, and the decision to adopt the term *Translation* as a more specific label for the complex activity of translating). Holz-Mänttäri's model starts from the reality of translation work and sees the translator at the centre of a process in which other actors (the client, the TT readers) play important roles that have a direct bearing on the way translation is carried out. In particular, the translator is seen as an expert in *text-design*, which he or she carries out taking into account all the product requirements as agreed between the parties involved. The skills required of translators are thus not only linguistic but include, among others, the ability to search for relevant information and to estimate the appropriate degree of cultural adaptation. Translation is thus seen by Holz-Mänttäri as a form of intercultural communication taking place in a social context, and particular emphasis is placed on the function served by the TT in the target context, in line with other theoretical approaches that emerged in Germany in the same years (e.g. *skopos* **theory**).

See also: **functionalist approaches**.

Transposition

This is a **translation technique** that involves a change of word class in the TT. For example, in translating the French *Après son retour . . .* with *After he comes back . . .*, a noun (*retour*) has been changed into a verb in English ('come back'). Whereas in this case the transposition is not obligatory (*After his return . . .* was possible), in other cases it is the only option available: cf. *Dès son lever . . . / As soon as he gets* or *got up . . .* (Vinay and Darbelnet [1958] 1995). Note that the term 'transposition' is also sometimes used as a synonym for (linguistic or cultural) transfer in general.

Triangulation

In **process-oriented research** on translation, the approach known as 'triangulation' tries to combine different data collection methods so as to test the hypotheses put forward by the researcher as regards the cognitive processes involved in translation on firmer empirical ground. This often implies complementing the qualitative data supplied by methods based on **verbal reporting** such as **Think-Aloud Protocols** with quantitative data obtained through other methods of observation. The triangulation approach is thus based on the convergence of different methodologies used to collect, elicit and interpret data (Jakobsen 1999; Alves 2003). The metaphor inspiring this approach assumes that 'navigating through uncharted waters requires several location points to establish one's position' and that therefore several instruments of data gathering and analysis can be simultaneously used to throw light on the nature of the translation process (Alves 2003: vii). The aim is that of reducing the risk that observations of a given phenomenon are 'mere methodological artefacts' (Jakobsen 1999: 19) and of ensuring that observational data are successfully validated. Besides verbal reporting, the data collection methods combined in studies adopting a triangulation approach include **keystroke logging**, eye-tracking (used to identify foci of attention on the part of translators, e.g. in a text displayed on a computer screen) and the recording of search processes in electronic environments.

Unbounded translation

In Catford (1965) a translation providing TL equivalents that cuts across the linguistic ranks observed in the SL. For example the phrase *acostarse* in Spanish translated *go to bed* in English can be seen to cut across the ranks of word (in Spanish) and group (in English).

See also: **rank-bound translation, shift**.

Unique items hypothesis

Recently included among the **universals of translation**, this hypothesis claims that the features which are 'untranslatable', i.e. unique to the TL or not occurring in the SL, tend to be proportionally underrepresented in translations as compared to non-translated texts. In other words, certain TL items or structures (e.g. pragmatic particles or rare lexicalizations) tend not to appear in translated texts because they have no direct counterpart in the SL. Studies investigating this hypothesis (e.g. Tirkkonen-Condit 2004) have been conducted mainly in relation to Finnish as a TL.

Unit of translation

The term refers to the entity which is taken to be processed by the translator at a given time during the process of translation. No agreement exists between scholars as to the nature and scope of such entities. A generally applicable definition depends on a variety of factors such as the translator him- or herself, the type of ST and the purpose of the translation (cf. Sorvali 2004). From a theoretical point of view, units of translation can be (and have been) postulated at different levels of linguistic description, although it remains to be seen whether in concrete translation acts translators really refer to such levels. At a syntactic level, units such as words, phrases or clauses can be considered. At the lexical and semantic level, meaning components (see **componential analysis**) or distinctions between the sense and reference of an utterance may be considered. At a functional level, notions such as **theme/rheme** come to the fore, while at a pragmatic level utterances can be seen as units realizing **speech acts**. The consideration of one or the other aspects will influence the way a text is seen to be segmented into units for purposes of translation. Within the same concrete translation act, units of processing may be seen to differ even markedly from one another. At one point the translator may be observed to consider possible TL lexical equivalents for an individual word, while later in the process s/he may enlarge the focus of attention or processing to longer stretches of text, possibly to consider their functional or pragmatic values (e.g. in the case of proverbs or fixed expressions).

Traditionally, scholars of translation have tended to equate the unit of translation with individual words (as in Newmark 1981) or with textual segments identified syntactically (Wilss 1982). Koller (1979) notes that the greater the structural difference between two languages, the longer the units are likely to be, and vice versa. Bassnett ([1980] 2002) emphasizes how whatever unit is considered, it is to be related to the text as a whole. Using process-related data obtained through **verbal reporting** or **keystroke logging**, some studies (cf. those reported on in Alves 2003) have looked at how, in concrete translation acts, source texts are segmented by translators.

Universal of translation

The term is used to indicate a linguistic feature typically observed in translated texts and occurring as a consequence of the translation process, i.e. independently from the pairs of languages involved and not as the result of **interference** between different linguistic systems. The search for universals began in the mid-1990s (see Baker 1996) drawing from developments in translation studies and the emergence of corpus linguistics in the previous decades. In translation studies, the attention of many scholars had moved away from the relationship between the ST and the TT to the translations themselves. Meanwhile, thanks to advances in computer storage capacities, language **corpora** of increasing size were being compiled, providing material where hypotheses about large-scale linguistic patterning could be tested. Among the first features to be hypothesized as universals of translation were **explicitation, simplification** and **normalization**. More recently, features such as **untypical collocations** and the under-representation of TL unique items (see **unique items hypothesis**) have been added to the list of hypothesized universals (cf. Mauranen and Kujamäki 2004; Mauranen 2007).

Most research on universals has been linguistically oriented and has relied on corpus-based methods, often starting from hypotheses that had been put forward in earlier, small-scale studies. There have also been suggestions that, beneath universals, there may be underlying processes of a cognitive nature, i.e. that translations present certain features as a result of the workings of the brain when it is engaged in translation. Such suggestions, however, still lack a rigorous application of cognitive models capable of giving reliable accounts of the translation process (Mauranen 2007: 37).

Over the years, both the concept of translation universals and the research approaches to be used in investigating them have been the object of intense debate. Further qualifications have been introduced in testing new and earlier hypothesis. Chesterman (2004b), for example, has pointed out that some hypotheses (e.g. explicitation) concern the relationship between source and translation, while others (e.g. normalization) mainly have to do with the difference between translated and non-translated texts. The former he calls *S-universals*, while the latter are termed *T-universals*.

Strong objections to the idea of translation universals have come from some scholars looking at translation from a historical point of view or drawing from socio-cultural research (cf. Mauranen 2007: 37). Such objections mainly regard the real comparability of translated and non-translated texts. Historically, there have been periods where a clear-cut distinction between translations and non-translations could not be drawn, which would make it problematic to make sweeping generalizations about *universal* features of translations. More generally, those scholars who see translation as an 'open field' (Tymoczko 2005) where different conceptualizations of translation co-exist tend to resist the idea that translated texts may be looked at in terms of universal features.

See also: **laws of translation, norms**.

Untypical collocations

Research carried out on comparable corpora has found that translated texts tend to display collocational patterns that deviate from the patterns observed in non-translated texts in the same language. Untypical collocations have thus been proposed as a hypothetical **universal of translation**. In particular, it has been found that, at both collocational and colligational level, translations tend to favour combinations that are infrequent or absent in non-translated texts. Conversely, translations seem to have fewer instances of combinations that are frequent in native TL texts.

See: **collocation, colligation**.

Verbal reporting

Verbal reporting is a method of data collection used in **process-oriented research** to investigate the cognitive and psycholinguistic processes involved in translation. It is based on the assumption that human cognition is information processing and that information is stored in memories with different capacities. Short-Term Memory (STM) stores information from the surrounding world, i.e. the information that is heeded or attended to. The amount of this particular kind of information stored in STM is limited. Long-Term Memory (LTM) is a vast collection of nodes which can be accessed either by recognition or by way of links associating nodes to others that have been already accessed. Both these processes bring information into STM. Information stored in STM remains accessible for further processing and for producing verbal reports. These can be of three types: introspective, retrospective and concurrent. In introspective reports, the subject of an experiment carries out a self-analysis of his/her thought processes. Retrospective reports are reports on thought processes that are given after the performance of a task. Concurrent reports take place at the same time as the task: here the subject is not asked to verbalize specific information but to think aloud (see **Think-Aloud Protocol**). Opinions on the respective validity of the various verbal report procedures differ, although concurrent reports are the method which has proved the most popular with translation researchers. Fraser (1996) sees immediate retrospections as superior in many respects, as they provide accounts that tend to be more structured and inferential, and thus more revealing than the concurrent verbalizations. Bernardini (2001), on the other hand, stresses that only concurrent verbalization (as opposed to *post hoc* verbalization) reflects the mental states of subjects. She also points out that, in order for the concurrent reports to be reliable, they must be strictly monological (cf. also Tirkkonen-Condit and Jääskeläinen 2000).

Voice-over

The term refers to a method of language transfer used in **audiovisual translation**. It consists in superimposing pre-recorded voicing in the TL on the original audio, which is however left audible in the background. It is mainly used for interviews, documentaries and other programmes in which a certain level of realism is required. In some markets, voice-over is also used for films and TV fiction as a cheaper alternative to lip-synchronized **dubbing**.

Word-for-word translation, see **free vs literal translation**.

Key Thinkers in Translation Studies

Andrew Chesterman

Largely following in the lead of **Gideon Toury** and the other translation scholars identified with descriptive and empirical approaches, Andrew Chesterman's work has developed the theoretical and methodological implications of those approaches. At the same time, he has attempted to trace the unifying themes and interests in the wider scenario of contemporary translation studies, looking at the possible connections between the disparate views on both translation and translation research adopted by theorists and applied researchers over the last few decades.

The reflection on the theoretical status of translation and translation research forms the basis of Chesterman's 1997 book *Memes of Translation*. The notion of the **meme**, taken from sociobiology (and, interestingly, also applied to translation by **Hans. J. Vermeer** in the same years), is used by Chesterman to account for how certain concepts and ideas about translation spread in society and across generations. A meme is a unit of cultural transmission or imitation (such as an idea, a catch-phrase or a fashion) which propagates from brain to brain, much as genes propagate from body to body via sperm or eggs (Chesterman 1997: 5). Translation is first of all a cognitive activity but it also takes place, as an event, in a given historical, social and cultural setting. Looking at views, ideas and concepts relating to translation as memes can be of help in describing how they are transmitted from individual to individual, thus establishing a link between the cognitive level of individuals and the social dimension of practice. In other words, certain memes, or perceptions, about translation spread, through social interaction, from individual to individual and define the way translation is generally talked about and practised. More specifically, Chesterman identifies certain ideas, called 'supermemes', exerting such influence that, over the centuries, they have come up again and again in discussion on the subject. These are the 'source-target' distinction, the concept of **equivalence**, the notion of untranslatability (see **translatability** and **translation**), the **free vs literal translation** opposition and the idea that 'all writing is translating'. Other examples of memes, of a more culturally and historically contingent nature than the 'supermemes', are the **norms** that govern translator behaviour in a given society or more restricted community. Translation strategies, seen as well-established ways to solve a given translation problem, can also be described as memes, propagated by one translator to another through formal training or by way of imitation (cf Chesterman 2000b).

Chesterman's treatment of translation norms, in particular, builds on Gideon Tory's elaboration of the notion. A norm is seen as 'a kind of consensus of opinion about what [translation] should be like, how it should be done'; it is therefore to be seen as a descriptive notion: 'a norm-statement describes what such consensus *is*, not what it *should* be' (Chesterman 1997: 3; orig. emphasis). Compared to Toury, Chesterman looks at norms from a broader perspective, taking into account not only process norms (as in Toury) but also product norms, so as to obtain a wider picture of the constraints operating on the practice and reception of translation. The two general kinds of norms are labelled by Chesterman *expectancy norms* and *professional norms*. The former are product norms; the latter have to do with the process of translation. Expectancy norms 'are established by the expectations of readers of a translation (of a given type) concerning what a translation (of that type) should be like' (Chesterman 1997: 64). They are governed by the prevailing translation tradition in a given culture and also, in part, by the form of **parallel texts** in the TL. They can be influenced by a variety of factors (such as **ideology** or the **power** relations between cultures) and ultimately represent the basis for evaluative judgements about translations. Professional norms are subordinate to expectancy norms in the sense that 'any process norm is determined by the nature of the end-product it will lead to' (Chesterman 1997: 67). The label professional norms is chosen by Chesterman to stress that the authorities that validate process norms are primarily the translators themselves. In particular, Chesterman (1997: 67–70) identifies three general higher-order professional norms. The *accountability norm* states that translators acts in such a way as to remain loyal to the ST authors, the translation commissioners, translators themselves, the prospective readership and other relevant parties. This is fundamentally an ethical norm concerning standards of professional integrity. The *communication norm* states that translators act so as to optimize communication between the parties involved. This is fundamentally a social norm. Finally, the *relation norm* states that translators act so as to establish 'an appropriate relation of similarity' (1997: 69) between ST and TT. This norm, which is specific to translation, implies that there is no predefined equivalence between ST and TT and that it is ultimately up to the translator to decide what kind of equivalence relation is appropriate given the context of the translation event. A translator who breaks one of these norms is usually seen as deserving criticism; if he or she rejects criticism, an argument about the appropriateness of the norm may start and, in the long run, this may also lead to a change in the norm itself.

Another major theme in Chesterman's work, with clear links to his discussion of norm theory, is the elaboration of a model capable of formulating explanatory hypotheses for the patterns of behaviour observed both in translators and in the readers of translations. Chesterman (2000a) reviews existing models of translation research and identifies three basic types, each associated with various theories and approaches: the 'comparative model' aligns STs and TTs and examines the correlations between them (e.g. in terms of equivalence); the 'process model' maps the different phases of the translation process over time (often characterizing translation as communication); finally, the 'causal model' sees translations 'as caused by antecedent conditions and as causing effects on readers' (2000a: 15). Chesterman's own preference is for the causal model, which he sees as the only one capable of allowing the formulation of explanatory hypotheses, i.e. of answering 'why' questions such as 'why is this translation like this?' or 'why do people react to this translation in this particular way?'. There are of course many possible levels of causation to be considered and different types of causes, from more to less deterministic. Rather than speak of causes, in the case of translation reference can be made to 'causal conditions' and a chain can be imagined where:

– socio-cultural conditions lead to a particular translation event;
– this event in turn leads to a particular translation act performed by an individual;
– the act results in a text with a specific linguistic profile;
– the text leads to some cognitive effects;
– the cognitive effects result in behavioural effects;
– these behavioural effects produce effects at the socio-cultural level.

Chesterman is careful to stress that this in only an idealization and that in reality no clear first cause or last effect can be discerned in such a chain. He also sees the translator at the centre of the model, as a crucial role is played by his or her cognitive processing. Translators 'have the final say' on the TT – it is their attitudes to factors such as norms or the purpose of the translation 'that ultimately count rather than these factors *per se*' (Chesterman 2000a: 26).

Chesterman's positions may certainly strike many scholars in translation studies as showing too much confidence on the possibility of applying methods of inquiry based on hypothesis testing to a complex phenomenon such as translation. On the other hand, by focusing attention on the many levels at which constraints on translation can be seen to operate and especially on the connections between such constraints, scholars such as Chesterman have played an essential role in delineating the scope of translation studies as a field of investigation, while making the most of its interdisciplinary nature. Chesterman (2004a; see also **translation studies**) himself sees the study of translation as primarily interested not in translated texts in isolation but in the relations that these texts establish with other entities of a disparate nature.

Essential reading

Chesterman, A. (1997), *Memes of Translation. The Spread of Ideas in Translation Theory.* Amsterdam/Philadelphia: Benjamins.

Chesterman, A. (2000a), 'A causal model for Translation Studies', in M. Olohan (ed.), *Intercultural Faultlines. Research Models in Translation Studies I. Textual and Cognitive Aspects.* Manchester: St Jerome, pp. 15–27.

Chesterman, A. (2004a), 'Translation as an object of reflection and scholarly discourse', in H. Kittel, A. P. Frank, N. Greiner, T. Hermans, W. Koller, J. Lambert and F. Paul (eds), *Übersetzung / Translation / Traduction.* Berlin: de Gruyter, pp. 93–100.

Basil Hatim and Ian Mason

Basil Hatim and Ian Mason have co-authored two influential books, published in 1990 and 1997, which show how advances in linguistics can be put to fruitful use in describing translating and translated texts. Whereas early linguistic or linguistically oriented approaches to translation (e.g. Nida 1964; Catford 1965) mainly focused on words and sentences as units of analysis, Hatim and Mason see translation as an act of communication performed at the level of text. Particular emphasis is also given in their analyses to the socio-cultural context in which translational communication unfolds, which they take to be 'probably a more important variable than the textual genre' (Hatim and Mason 1990: 13) itself. Their text-linguistic approach is thus couched in a larger pragmatic and semiotic framework seen as capable of accounting for the motivations lying behind text processing in general and translation in particular. Their approach to text processing is elaborated by analysing a wealth of examples taken from authentic texts of different types.

In their first book, *Discourse and the Translator* (1990), Hatim and Mason start from the assumption that identifying the register of a text is an essential but insufficient step in analysing the text for translation purposes. Register analysis, in particular, is seen as useful in helping the translator as reader to reconstruct the situational variables relating to a text, which they identify adopting a Hallidayan approach. Thus register helps to pinpoint the variety of language used in particular texts (medical, legal, etc. – Halliday's *field*) or in particular circumstances (e.g. between friends, at work, etc. – *tenor*) and distinguished by particular choice of vocabulary or style (*mode*). This, however, is felt to be insufficient for the identification of the communicative intentions of texts, which Hatim and Mason see as a crucial factor in text processing aimed at translation. As an example, they quote and analyse the initial passage of an article on dental care taken from a journal (Hatim and Mason 1990: 55–57). Seen, from the point of view of register, the article would be characterized as a text about dental care (field) written by an academic for semi-specialist readers (tenor) largely according to the conventions of academic writing (mode). Such an analysis, however, would reveal little about the communicative intention of the author. The first sentence of the article, in particular, reads as follows: *Oral health care does not have the makings of a dramatic issue.* Only by going beyond an analysis of register can it be shown that with this first sentence the author is in fact announcing a different point of view (i.e. that dental care *is* an important issue). Both this sentence and the whole text, in other words, perform some kind of action that can only be described by recourse to other dimensions of text and discourse processing, namely **pragmatics** and semiotics. Reference to the pragmatic dimension helps in characterizing meaning as something which is negotiated between text producers and receivers and not as a static entity independent of human processing. Considering the semiotic dimensions helps in characterizing the mutual relationships between texts or parts of texts as signs (i.e. as meaningful entities). Thus, to go back to the example above, the pragmatic force attached to the sentence will also derive, semiotically, from its positioning at the beginning of a string of other sentences. The relevance of all this for the translator lies both in the ability to perceive intended meaning and in the ability to recognize the cases in which 'expression of intended meaning is subject to subtle variation between SL and TL text' (Hatim and Mason 1990: 57).

As a further means of describing texts in terms of their interactional and communicative aims, Hatim and Mason (1990: Chap. 8) elaborate their own **text typology**, which is also an attempt at accommodating the extreme diversity and multi-functionality found in real texts – a feature that, for them, was not reflected in previous translation-oriented typologies. The basis for Hatim and Mason's typology is the assumption that any given text is the concrete realization of an underlying ideal type characterized by an overall rhetorical purpose, and that this purpose is the most salient in relation to the **context**. Three main types are identified, *exposition*, *argumentation* and *instruction*, each having two or three main variants. Exposition is defined as a text type presenting, in a non-evaluative manner, concepts ('conceptual exposition'), objects ('description') or events ('narration'). Argumentation is the evaluative presentation of concepts; it can take the form of 'through-argumentation' (i.e. citation of thesis to be argued through) or 'counter-argumentation' (citation of thesis to be opposed). Lastly, instruction is a text type focusing on the formation of future behaviour, and can be 'with option' (as in advertising) or 'without option' (as in contracts). The implications for translation of such a classification can be summarized as follows: the text is the structural unit that informs the translator's decisions about choices at other levels (lexical and syntactic); these decisions are largely taken in light of the rhetorical purpose of the text, which is also the basis for the **assessment** of translated texts.

In their next book, *The Translator as Communicator* (1997), Hatim and Mason refine their approach, proposing a series of case studies aimed at testing its usefulness beyond the traditional distinction between literary and non-literary translation or even between translation and interpreting. One particular aspect that is further developed in this second book is **ideology** (Hatim and Mason 1997: Chap. 9), seen as one of the factors that motivate linguistic modes of expression. In particular, Hatim and Mason draw a distinction between the 'ideology of translating' and the 'translation of ideology'. The former is related to the ideological consequences generated by translation itself and in particular by the choice of a given general mode of text transfer (e.g. **domestication** as opposed to **foreignization**). Hatim and Mason stress that it is not a certain mode of transfer as such that is ideologically slanted, but rather that the mode of transfer acquires a certain ideological character depending on the socio-cultural situation of the TL. Thus, a domesticating strategy can be seen as adhering to prevailing values when it is used in a translation from a minority culture into a dominant culture, but the same strategy can be seen as a form of 'resistance' when the translation is from a dominant into a minority culture. As regards the translation of ideology, Hatim and Mason look at cases where translators handle the ideological features of STs in markedly different ways, largely as the result of the degree of 'mediation' observed in the text, i.e. the extent to which 'translators intervene in the transfer process, feeding their own knowledge and beliefs into the processing of a text' (1997: 147). In particular, Hatim and Mason show how essentially linguistic analytical concepts (e.g. cohesion, lexical choice and Hallidayan transitivity) can arrive at the identification of such mediation, provided the linguistic evidence available 'is part of a discernible trend' (1997: 147).

Essential reading

Hatim, B. and Mason, I. (1990), *Discourse and the Translator*. London/New York: Longman.

Hatim, B. and Mason, I. (1997), *The Translator as Communicator*. London/New York: Routledge.

James S. Holmes

The work of James S. Holmes (1924–1986) has exerted an enormous influence on the development and consolidation of translation studies as a discipline in its own right. An American who moved to the Netherlands in the late 1940s, Holmes was a poet, literary scholar, translator and translation theorist, each of his interests feeding the others without confusing the respective roles of practice and theory. After starting work as a lecturer at the Department of General Literary Studies of the University of Amsterdam in the 1960s, he grew an interest in the study of literary translation, at the time a neglected area of research, and gradually built an international network of collaborations which eventually led to the establishment of a circle of scholars (including **Gideon Toury**, Itamar Even-Zohar, Anton Popovič and André Lefevere) who, in the next decades, gradually developed and propagated a new paradigm of translation research (see **descriptive translation studies**).

Holmes' own work followed two major strands. On the one hand, he investigated issues of literary translation, and particularly the translation of poetry. On the other, he engaged in discussions on the status of translation as a discipline of academic enquiry and on issues of research methodology, which he believed should be made to fit a view of translation as a distinct field of investigation. Holmes' works on literary translation, mostly concerned with the translation of poetry (see the papers collected in Holmes 1988), try to characterize the literary and socio-cultural constraints operating on the decisions taken by translators at the formal, linguistic level. Holmes' best-known and most influential works, however, are certainly those where he reflected on the status of translation as a discipline of inquiry. The history of such works is in itself an interesting case of how ideas can slowly and gradually be disseminated in a discipline until they reach a tipping point after which their influence on the discipline as a whole becomes manifest.

Holmes' ideas on 'The name and nature of translation studies' were first presented in a paper of the same title delivered at the Third International Congress of Applied Linguistics, held in Copenhagen in

1972. The paper had very limited circulation for well over 10 years, until it appeared, in slightly expanded form, in a collection of works published after Holmes' death (Holmes 1988). In this paper, Holmes presented a general framework for the discipline of 'Translation Studies' (a name he himself proposed), delineating its scope and structure and spelling out its objectives. This framework was intended to present translation studies as a full-scale discipline concerned with 'the complex of problems clustered round the phenomena of translating and translations' (Holmes 1988: 67). It was later presented by Toury (1995) as Holmes' 'map' of translation studies, which further contributed to its dissemination.

In keeping with his view of translation studies as an essentially empirical discipline, Holmes' paper identifies two main objectives for the discipline: '(1) to describe the phenomena of translating and translation(s) as they manifest in the world, and (2) to establish general principles by means of which these phenomena can be explained and predicted' (Holmes 1988: 71). The two branches of 'pure research' that Holmes sees as concerning themselves with these objectives are, respectively, *descriptive translation studies* and *theoretical translation studies*. The descriptive branch is the one that maintains close contact with empirical phenomena and is seen by Holmes (1988: 72–73) as comprising three major kinds of research:

- *product-oriented* research is the area that describes existing translations comparatively, i.e. analysing various translations of the same text (in one or more languages) in relation to one specific historical period or text type;
- *function-oriented* research is the area interested in the description of the function served by translated texts in the TL socio-cultural situation and pursues such questions as which texts are (or are not) translated in a given period and place;
- *process-oriented* research is the area interested in describing what goes on in the mind of translators as they translate.

The other main branch of 'pure' translation studies, *theoretical translation studies* or *translation theory*, is seen by Holmes as the one that uses the results obtained in descriptive research and combines them with the information available from related fields (e.g. linguistics, literary studies or information theory) so as 'to evolve principles, theories, and models which will serve to explain and predict what translating and translations are and will be' (1988: 73). The ultimate goal of translation studies is to establish a general theory capable of explaining all the various phenomena falling within the domain of translating and translations – an ambitious goal that Holmes sees as attainable by the elaboration of *partial* theories of restricted scope. In particular, Holmes (1988: 73–76) identifies six partial theories:

- *Medium-restricted theories* are concerned with the particular medium used for translation, i.e. humans or machines or a mixture of the two; human translation, in particular can further be subdivided in oral translation (or interpreting) and written translation.
- *Area-restricted theories* deal with particular languages or cultures; more specifically, theories can be 'language-pair restricted' (e.g. involving English and Spanish only) or 'language-group restricted' (e.g. a theory of translation between Romance and Germanic languages); by the same token, they could be restricted to particular pairs or groups of cultures (e.g. a theory of translation between Swiss and Belgian cultures or a theory of translation in contemporary Western culture). This is also the area having close affinities with **contrastive analysis** and stylistics.
- *Rank-restricted theories* are concerned with translation at specific linguistic ranks or levels. Holmes himself notes how, traditionally, theories of translation have looked mainly at the levels of words and sentences, ignoring macro-structural aspects at higher levels such as text; his prediction that text-rank theories would be pursued in years to come has proved successful.
- *Text-type restricted theories* deal with the problems specific to given test types or genres.
- *Time-restricted theories* deal either with contemporary translation or with the translation of texts from past historical periods.

- *Problem-restricted theories* are concerned with specific aspects of translation, such as the notion of **equivalence** in translation, the translation of proper names or the translation of metaphor.

The third and final branch of translation studies identified by Holmes is that of *applied translation studies*, which Holmes sees as falling outside the scope of pure research. Within this branch Holmes (1988: 78–79) identifies four areas of scholarly interest:

- *translation teaching*, and particularly the development of appropriate teaching methods, testing techniques, and curricula for the training of professional translators;
- *translation aids*, i.e. translator-oriented lexicographical and terminological resources;
- *translation policy*, defined by Holmes (1988: 79) as the task of rendering informed advice in the definition of 'the place and role of translators, translating, and translations in society';
- *translation criticism*, seen as an area where contact between scholars and critics could help reduce intuitive judgements.

Holmes stresses that the interaction between the three branches (descriptive, theoretical and applied) is not unidirectional but dialectical, 'each of the three branches supplying materials for the other two, and making use of the findings that they in turn provide it' (1988: 78).

Holmes' map of translation studies as delineated in his seminal paper of 1972 has played a key role in defining the scope of the discipline and establishing a frame of reference for subsequent debate concerning both the internal structure of the field and the nature of its connections with neighbouring disciplines. In many respects, Holmes' structuring of translation studies appears still capable of accommodating developments that Holmes himself could only envisage, such as **process-oriented research** or the advances in computerized **translation tools**. On the other hand, some scholars (e.g. Ulrych 1999) have in recent years noted the unbalance existing between the two 'pure' branches on the one hand and the applied branch on the other, with the applied side having been somewhat disregarded by those who more closely followed Holmes' programme of research. Other recent developments which either do not find a proper place in Holmes' map or seem to fall outside its scope are the increasing attention given to translators as mediating agents motivated by cultural and ideological factors (as in **cultural studies approaches**) and the increased autonomy of interpreting, today seen by some scholars as a separate, parallel field to translation studies.

Essential reading
Holmes, J. H. (1988), *Translated! Papers on Literary Translation and Translation Studies*. Amsterdam: Rodopi.
Toury, G. (1995), *Descriptive Translation Studies and Beyond*. Amsterdam/Philadelphia: Benjamins [see especially Part One].

Juliane House

Translation **assessment** of an evaluative nature has often been considered to be based on anecdotal and impressionistic criteria. Beyond the level of mere TL grammaticality, at which assessment can be equated with more or less mechanical forms of error analysis, translation assessment looks at aspects such as style, function and rhetorical organization. One of the first systematic models of translation assessment has been elaborated by the German scholar Juliane House, whose book *A Model for Translation Quality Assessment* first appeared in 1977. The model underwent substantial revision, especially in its 'operational' component, in the following years and was presented in its revised form in House (1997). House's model can be seen to have played a pioneering role in many respects, especially as regards the recognition of contextual features and the role played by different types of **equivalence**.

House sees a translated text as bound both to the ST and to the TL recipients' communicative conditions. The basic aim of her model is to delineate a framework for equivalence between ST and TT and to identify the dimensions on the basis of which assessment can be carried out. These dimensions take into account a variety of factors: extra-linguistic circumstances; the connotative and aesthetic values of texts; the TL audience; and the TL textual and linguistic usage norms, to be identified through the empirical observation of **parallel texts** and through **contrastive analysis** looking at both rhetorical and pragmatic aspects. As it depends on such factors, equivalence is not a static but a dynamic and relative notion and the translator is seen as having to make a choice in terms of the type of equivalence to be privileged for a given ST.

A key feature of House's model is the analysis of the ST, which is aimed at identifying the main function of the text. This function is seen as the pivotal factor around which assessment takes place, as equivalence between texts is established primarily in functional terms. In previous models of assessment (e.g. Reiss 1971) the function of texts was identified mainly in relation to the type of language observed in them, and texts were categorized in relation to the prevailing language function they were seen to realize. House's model is not aimed at the identification of text types but, rather, at delineating the dimensions of texts along which assessment can be carried out. In her first version of the model (House 1977), these dimensions are described using a Hallidayan framework, where language is seen to realize three main functions: an ideational function related to the expression of content, and interpersonal function related to the ways in which participants in communication interact and a textual function related to how language is used in order to serve the previous two functions. This is used by House to characterize the components of the context of situation in relation to any given text, or what she calls the 'situational dimensions' of texts. A total of eight dimensions is identified, having to do with aspects relating to the language users (e.g. geographical origin and social class) and to language use (e.g. the topic of a text and the type of interaction the text is designed for). These situational dimensions constitute the set of parameters against which assessment is carried out. In particular, assessment consists in (1) determining the textual profile of the ST on the basis of the situational dimensions, and (2) comparing the ST with the TT so as to observe the degree of match between their textual profiles. The final 'statement of quality' is based on the degree of match between the situational dimensions, but also takes into account 'non-dimensional mismatches' such as errors in conveying denotative meaning and breaches of the TL system.

In her revised version of the model, House (1997) essentially overhauls the analytical categories used for determining textual profiles. Still largely remaining within a Hallidayan framework, she now analyses texts in terms of register, looking at field (i.e. roughly, the subject matter), tenor (i.e. who takes part in the communication) and mode (i.e. the channel of communication and the ways in which interaction is established, e.g. through the use of imperative or interrogative sentences). This is complemented by the notion of **genre**, which House sees as suitable for relating a given individual text to the class of texts with which it shares a common communicative purpose. In particular, the notion of register is used to analyse texts at the micro-contextual level of linguistic choices, while genre is used to connect a text with the macro-context of the linguistic and cultural community. As in the previous version of the model, the aim is to identify a textual profile and then use this as a yardstick for translation assessment.

The textual profile as identified at the analytical stage of House's model essentially characterizes the function of a text. In considering it for translation assessment, House notes, however, that another factor must be taken into account, namely, the type of general **translation strategy** required by a text. Whereas earlier model of translation assessments looked at *text* types, holding the strategy chosen for translation as a constant, House believes that this strategy is a fundamental factor and that its role must be acknowledged, so as to accommodate factors of a processual nature in the framework for assessment. The two general translation types identified by House, on the basis of an empirical observation of translated texts, are *overt* and *covert translation*. The distinction is introduced in House (1977) and then refined in the later version of the model.

An overt translation is one that presents the text explicitly as a translation. Two essential types of source text lead to such a translation (House 1997: 66–69): a text closely associated with a historical occasion (e.g. a speech delivered by a prominent political figure) or what House calls a 'timeless' (1997: 66) text, i.e. a text of literary status that, while, transmitting a message of general significance is also clearly source-culture specific. With these types of texts, a direct match of the original ST function is not possible, as translation entails a displacement of the text which makes its original function lose the relevance it had in the original context (which, incidentally, can also happen in the SL context when the reception of the text is far removed along the temporal axis). The task of the translator of such texts is, for House, that of ensuring that the TL reader has access to the cultural and contextual 'discourse world' of the original. In the TT, in other words, the translator aims at matching a 'second level function' (House 1997: 67). In particular, House suggests that for texts linked to specific historical occasions the translator should abstain from any changes aimed at finding equivalents for culture-specific geographical, temporal or social-class markers. For literary texts, however, she accepts that TL cultural equivalents for such markers may in some cases be proposed. For example, expressions in a given SL dialect might be replaced with a TL dialect (House 1997: 68), but cases such as these are often bound to lead to insoluble equivalence problems. Covert translation, on the other hand, is the strategy leading to the creation of a translated text that 'enjoys the status of an original source text in the target culture' (1997: 69). In particular, a covert translation is one that reproduces the function of the ST where this function has no particular ties to the source culture. Texts that lead to a covert translation include scientific and economic texts, tourist brochures, journalistic texts and in general all 'authorless texts or texts that have dispensable authors' (House 1997: 163). The original and its covert translation need not, for House, be equivalent at the linguistic, textual and register level. At these levels the translator may legitimately manipulate the original using what House calls a *cultural filter*, i.e. a motivated intervention on the ST aimed at adjusting the translation in terms of the usage norms and the stylistic conventions prevalent in the TL community.

The overt/covert distinction is added to the parameters relating to the linguistic-textual profile so as to compose the general framework for the assessment of translated texts. Overt and covert translations differ in terms of the equivalence established between ST and TT. In particular, covert translation may be seen to be equivalent in terms of the 'primary level function' of the text, i.e. it serves in the TL the same function as in the SL. Overt translation, on the other hand, only 'serves a secondary level function', i.e. one that is different from that of the ST. Particular importance is attached by House in the revised version of her model to the *cultural filter* that, in covert translation, she sees as operating so that equivalence of primary level function is established. The cultural filter is what enables the translator to treat rhetorical and stylistic aspects such as directness, explicitness and reliance on verbal routines of formulas, adapting them to the conventions observed in the TL for a given genre. These aspects of cross-cultural pragmatics are of primary importance in translation, but as House herself acknowledges (1997: 115f.), empirical studies in this area are still scarce and constitute a possible fruitful direction of future research on translation.

Essential reading
House, J. (1977), *A Model for Translation Quality Assessment*. Tübingen: Narr.
House, J. (1997), *Translation Quality Assessment. A Model Revisited*. Tübingen: Narr.

Peter Newmark

In the English-speaking world, Peter Newmark has played a crucial role in the development of translation as an academic discipline and a subject for training at academic level. Born in Czechoslovakia, he moved to Britain in his early childhood and there he studied Modern Languages at Trinity College, Cambridge. After World War II he began his lifelong career as a teacher of modern languages, which culminated in 1974 with his appointment as Professor of Translation at the Polytechnic of Central London, where he introduced the first courses in Translation Theory together with training on both literary and non-literary translation. In the same years he started contributing articles on translation to *The Linguist* and in 1981 he published *Approaches to Translation*, a book that in the following years was adopted in translator training courses all over the world. His second book, *A Textbook of Translation* (1988), again proved popular with translator trainers thanks to its wealth of examples and the wide range of topics treated in it.

The teaching and practice of translation play a significant role in Peter Newmark's view on translation, which is firmly established within a linguistically oriented approach but is prepared to acknowledge the influence of considerations that go beyond linguistics, embracing primarily the procedural aspects of translation but also touching on issues such as the translator's moral responsibilities. Translation theory, for Newmark (1981: 37),

> precipitates a methodology concerned with making the translator pause and think, with producing a natural text or a conscious deviation from a natural text or a closest natural equivalent, with sensitizing him against howlers and false cognates, but not being afraid to recognize true cognates.

Newmark's theory thus concerns, in essence, the methodology of translation, which he sees as the identification and description of the procedures that are more likely to help the translator in providing an answer to what he considers to be the central issue of translation: when to translate 'freely' and when to translate 'literally'. The identification of an appropriate method of translation is seen by Newmark as resting on the consideration of a variety of factors, starting from the language functions realized by the ST through to the role of contextual factors and the relative importance of ST author and TT readers, an aspect which he considers as playing a fundamental role.

Reacting against the emphasis given to the role of TT readers (and the consequent equation of translation with communication) that he sees as typical of some contemporary approaches (e.g. **Eugene A. Nida**'s), Newmark (1981) proposes a distinction between two general methods of translation, *communicative* and *semantic* translation: the former 'attempts to produce on its readers an effect as close as possible to that obtained on the readers of the original'; the latter 'attempts to render, as closely as the semantic and syntactic structures of the second language allow, the exact contextual meaning of the original' (Newmark 1981: 39). In other words, while communicative translation recognizes the importance of catering for the TT reader's needs, semantic translation is a mode of translation intended to acknowledge the authority of the ST author. In particular, communicative translation is presented by Newmark as suited for all those texts (the majority) where originality of expression is not an important aspect. Semantic translation, on the other hand, is presented as the method to be preferred for texts in which the form is as important as the content, e.g. great speeches, autobiographical and literary works, but also philosophical, scientific and technical texts showing originality of expression.

Newmark's distinction echoes Nida's opposition between formal and dynamic equivalence in translation, where dynamic equivalence is based on the principle of equivalent effect. Newmark's focus, however, is not on the effect to be achieved by the translated text but, rather, on the orientation of translation in terms of accuracy. His semantic translation is meant to accurately reproduce the meanings of the ST as presented by its author, while communicative translation is intended to accurately reproduce the communicative significance and force of the ST, thereby insisting on the TL context and readers. For Newmark, **equivalent effect** is an 'important intuitive principle' (1988: 49) but it is also ultimately illusory, especially 'if the [source] text is out of TL space and time' (1981: 69). It is seen as having a degree of application to any type of text, but not the same degree of importance (Newmark 1988: 49).

The two general methods of communicative and semantic translation are set by Newmark against the functions served by the text to be translated, which he describes by resorting to Karl Bühler's distinction between expressive, informative and vocative uses of language (see **language functions**). In general, the more important the language of a text, i.e. the more prominent the expressive function, the more closely, i.e. 'semantically', the text has to be translated. Conversely, the more informative or vocative the language of the ST, the more 'communicative' the translation. The two methods, semantic and communicative, could thus be said to give prominence on SL words and TL context respectively, and the role of theory is for Newmark essentially that of assisting translators in choosing either method or in reaching the right compromise between them on the basis of the relevant factors in the translation situation. Within this framework, a particular aspect emphasized by Newmark in more recent years is the obligation of translators to consider their task as ultimately responding neither to authors nor to readers, but rather to 'universal truth', so as to be prepared to identify and gloss any expression of prejudice in the texts they translate.

Newmark's insistence on translation methodology and the enormous wealth of practical examples of translation techniques and procedures that he gives in his writings must then be interpreted in light of his essentially utilitarian view of theory and his insistence on translation practice as a skill and an art. This lends to his discussion of translation a strongly prescriptive bias of the kind which many scholars of the next generation have tried to avoid. Much as with Nida's work, however, Newmark's ideas on translation continue to be of relevance for several aspects of the current scholarly debate on translation.

Essential reading
Newmark, P. (1981), *Approaches to Translation*. Oxford: Pergamon.
Newmark, P. (1988), *A Textbook of Translation*. New York/London: Prentice Hall.

Eugene A. Nida

Eugene A. Nida's theory of translation, elaborated over the two decades following 1945, is essentially a result of his work on Bible translation, but his ideas have had a profound effect on thinking about translation in general, in many ways dominating the field up until the consolidation of functional, cultural and historical-descriptive approaches in the 1980s. Nida's work has a firm linguistic grounding but at the same time insists on the communicative aspects of translation, emphasizing the reception of target readers and the ensuing dynamism linked to any act of meaning transfer across languages and cultures. Indeed, he makes a point of talking about *receptor* language instead of *target* language so as to stress the fact that in translation a message is 'received' by readers rather than 'shot' at a target. A full-length account of Nida's theory of translation is presented in *Towards a Science of Translating* (Nida 1964); the book was followed a few years later by another much-quoted volume (this time having a more pedagogical focus) co-authored with Charles R. Taber: *The Theory and Practice of Translation* (Nida and Taber 1969).

Translation is for Nida to be equated with the reproduction of a message in the TL. As such, it should give priority to the transfer of meaning over formal correspondence with the SL, to a consideration of contextual meaning over fixed semantic correspondences, and to TL naturalness and acceptability, this last aspect being closely associated with a consideration of the type of audience the translation is addressed to. This view of translation is based on a model of communication that sees language as the communication of a message which is encoded by the sender and then decoded by the receiver. In translation, a transfer mechanism is posited by Nida whereby the decoding of messages in the SL can be transformed so as to become a source for the encoding in the TL. The ethnolinguistic dimension of the model gives emphasis to the receiving end and in particular to the cultural and temporal differences often existing between STs and TTs.

Based on the general model briefly sketched above, translating is seen by Nida as a process involving there fundamental stages: ST analysis, transfer and restructuring in the TL. At the analysis stage, the first step in translating, the translator considers the grammatical relationships between ST constituents, the referential meaning of ST semantic units and the connotative values of these units. The aim of the grammatical analysis is that of transforming the surface structures of the ST into underlying core structures, a move that can facilitate transfer into another language. In particular, the core structures identified by grammatical analysis are the *kernels*, i.e. 'basic structural elements out of which the language builds its elaborate surface structures' (Nida and Taber 1969: 39). These are seen to belong to four basic structural classes: objects (e.g. *man*, *dog*, *tree*), events (*run*, *walk*, like), abstracts (divided into: qualitative: *red*, *big*; quantitative: *many*, *twice*; intensive: *too*, *very*; and spatio-temporal: *here*, *that*) and relationals (functioning as markers of the relations between other terms: *at*, *by*, *because*). The process used to transform elements of the surface structure into kernels is labelled *back-transformation*. Used on simple phrases, this process may help in clarifying the relations between individual elements. So, for example, reducing to kernel level the grammatical constructions formed by two nouns or pronouns connected by *of* may reveal the diversity of relations that this structure expresses. Examples include (cf. Nida and Taber 1969: 36–37):

(a) the will of God – God wills
(b) the foundation of the world – (God) creates the world
(c) the riches of grace – (God) shows grace
(d) remission of sins – (God) forgives (the people's) sin

Once back-transformation is applied to longer stretches of text, and meaningful relations between the kernels have been identified, a *kernel sentence* is arrived at, that is, a simple, declarative sentence ready for transfer into another language. For example, the sentence *John . . . preached the baptism of repentance unto the forgiveness of the sins* can be segmented into the following near-kernel structures

(Nida [1969] 1989: 84–85):

> (1) John preached (the message) (to the people) (2) John baptized (the people) (3) (the people) repented of (their) sins (4) (God) forgave (the people) (their) sins (5) (the people) sinned

After the relations between the kernels are spelled out, the sentence could be reformulated as *John preached that the people should repent and be baptized so that God would forgive the evil they had done*, or, using a form of direct address, *John preached, Repent and be baptized so that God will forgive the evil you have done*, to be used as the basis for translation. Nida's approach to grammatical analysis is the aspect which shows more clearly how his theory of translation was influenced by the linguistic theories prevalent in the 1950s and 1960s. In particular, the notion of kernels is based on Noam Chomsky's generative-transformational grammar, a model of language presenting surface sentences as the result of various levels of transformation operated on 'deep structure', an underlying structural level common to all languages.

At the level of semantics, the analysis stage of translation looks at the referential and connotative meaning of words. In both cases the role of context in resolving the potential ambiguity of words is considered essential. Nida presents various methods of semantic analysis, such as looking at the hierarchical relationships between meanings (Nida and Taber 1969: 68f.) or performing **componential analysis** (Nida 1964: 84f.), a method aimed at discovering and organizing the semantic components of words.

The transfer stage is seen by Nida as taking place at near-kernel level, that is, the level at which relations between units are more easily identified and languages exhibit the greatest degree of similarity. At the semantic level, this is the stage where the componential features identified during analysis can be redistributed onto the units that will then form the basis for the restructuring stage. Redistribution of the semantic components can be 'complete', as in the transfer of idioms, 'analytical' as when the word *disciples* is translated with elements saying something like 'those who followed him', or it may involve a 'synthesis', as when *brothers and sisters* is translated with a word meaning 'siblings'.

At the stage of restructuring the translator decides on the final TL form of the translation. In particular, at this stage Nida distinguishes between two basic orientations in translating, both aimed at finding the closest possible equivalents in the TL but differing in their focus of attention. *Formal equivalence* is the mode oriented at the form and content of the source-language message. *Dynamic equivalence* is the mode oriented at the target receivers: it is the 'the closest natural equivalent to the source-language message' (Nida 1964: 166), where 'natural' means that the translation must fit the target language and culture as a whole, the context of the particular message and the target audience. Although he acknowledges that formal equivalence as a mode of translation may be suitable for certain types of messages and audiences, Nida clearly equates successful translation with one where dynamic equivalence predominates, as evidenced by what he presents as the four basic requirements of a translation (Nida 1964: 164): (1) making sense, (2) conveying the spirit and manner of the original, (3) having a natural and easy form of expression and (4) producing a similar response (see **equivalent effect**).

Nida's insistence on the reception pole in translation and the naturalness to be ensured in target texts has probably been influenced by his work on Bible translation (an area in which he has been a firm opponent of earlier approaches advocating formal correspondence); seen from a larger perspective, his theory can be characterized as the first linguistically based consolidation of views of translation as communication – one stating a strong case for all the approaches that, throughout the history of thinking on translation, had variously been presented as alternatives to literalness or faithfulness. Nida's insistence on equivalence of effect has later been criticized as an impossible ideal, on account of the fact the translation invariably involves a loss of the meanings and context associated with the ST and that response to a text is hardly the same in two different cultures and times. By the same token, his treatment of meaning may seem too confident on the possibility securing it on a 'scientific' description.

These reservations notwithstanding, Nida's work can be considered a landmark for at least two reasons. First, his theory of translation has been among the first to analyse in a systematic fashion translation problems and the way they are linked to issues of style and culture. Second, Nida's insistence on the dynamic character of translation can be seen as a plausible answer to the question of **translatability**, of which it has contributed to emphasize the relativistic nature. As Nida wrote back in the 1960s:

> descriptions or definitions of translating are not served by deterministic rules; rather, they depend on probabilistic rules. One cannot therefore state that a particular translation is good or bad without taking into consideration a myriad factors, which in turn must be weighted in a number of different ways, with a number of appreciably different answers. (Nida 1964: 164)

Words such as 'probabilistic' and 'factor' and the emphasis on the 'difference' in responses to translated texts are still very much at the centre of the debate on translation more than forty years on.

Essential reading

Nida, E. A. (1964), *Toward a Science of Translating: With Special Reference to Principles and Procedures Involved in Bible Translating*. Leiden: E. J. Brill.

Nida, E. A. ([1969] 1989), 'Science of Translation', in A. Chesterman (ed.), *Readings in Translation Theory*. Helsinki: Finn Lectura, pp. 80–98. Originally published in: *Language*, 45(3), 1969, pp. 483–498.

Nida, E. A. and Taber, C. R. (1969), *The Theory and Practice of Translation*. Leiden: E. J. Brill.

Mary Snell-Hornby

The UK-born linguist Mary Snell-Hornby has been among the earliest proponents of an interdisciplinary approach in years in which the study of translation was still widely considered to belong to the realm of either linguistics or literary studies, with little communication between the two sides as regards possible combinations of approaches and methods. Building on a vast experience as both a translator and a teacher of translation in Germany, in 1988 Snell-Hornby published the book *Translation Studies. An Integrated Approach*, with the aim of showing how some concepts developed in linguistics could indeed be put to beneficial use in the analysis of literary translation. At the same time, the book laid the groundwork for an approach intended to grant independent status to translation studies as a discipline. This was an objective that various scholars (such as **James H. Holmes**) had also been pursuing in the previous years, although largely unbeknownst to the others on account of the still fragmented situation of the field. In the subsequent years Snell-Hornby has played a fundamental role in the consolidation of translation studies as a field in its own right and she has also been one of the strongest advocates of its fundamentally interdisciplinary nature.

In her 1988 book (revised in 1995), Snell-Hornby proposes a categorization of texts aimed at signalling the system of relationships among the text themselves and the relevant criteria for translation. Any given text is seen by Snell-Hornby as a complex multidimensional whole and the concrete realization of an ideal **prototype**. More specifically, Snell-Hornby's categorization takes the form of a stratificational model proceeding from the most general to the most specific level. In particular, the model incorporates the following levels, each presented as a cline with no clear demarcations:

A. the three general conventional areas of translation: literary, general language, special language;
B. the prototypical basic text types, ranging from the Bible through to theatre works and films, poetry, literature, light fiction, newspaper

texts, advertising, legal texts, medical texts and scientific and technological texts;

C. the non-linguistic disciplines of relevance for translation, including cultural history, socio-cultural and area studies and special subjects;

D. the aspects and criteria relevant for the translation process, to be related to:
  1. the scope of interpretation of the ST, which is broader at the literary pole and narrower at the special-language pole;
  2. the conceptual adherence between ST and TT, seen as looser at the literary pole and closer at the special-language pole;
  3. the communicative function of the TT, which becomes strictly informative towards the special-language pole;

E. the areas of linguistics relevant for translation, including historical linguistics (literary pole), text linguistics and pragmatics and terminology (special-language pole).

Translation-oriented analyses of texts (aimed either at performing or assessing translation) should, for Snell-Hornby, proceed from 'the top down'. In other words, strategies of translation can be developed proceeding from general observations as regards area of specialization, language variety and style of the text, down to individual grammatical and lexical items. The interdisciplinary nature of translation derives from this multiple dimensions found in texts.

Snell-Hornby's model has been among the first to point to the specificity of translation as both an activity and a field of inquiry. In drawing attention to the 'web of relationships' (Snell Hornby [1988] 1995: 36) translation is concerned with, she has been prescient of many developments that were to come in the discipline in the following two decades, as the attention of scholars moved from an exclusive preoccupation with issues of **equivalence** to the study of the several various constraints acting on translational phenomena. In her later work Snell-Hornby herself has focused on areas such the translation of multimodal texts and **theatre translation** (see e.g. Snell-Hornby 1996, 2006), which had hardly been investigated prior to the

1980s. Of particular interest is also her more recent book *The Turns of Translation Studies* (2006), which charts the development of the discipline in the last few decades, critically assessing the significance of its various 'turns' and (real or assumed) changes of paradigm.

Essential reading

Snell-Hornby, M. ([1988] 1995), *Translation Studies. An Integrated Approach*. Amsterdam/Philadelphia: Benjamins.

Snell-Hornby, M. (2006), *The Turns of Translation Studies*. Amsterdam/Philadelphia: Benjamins.

Gideon Toury

Within the disciplinary framework delineated by **James H. Holmes**, whose work he has greatly contributed to disseminate, the Israeli scholar Gideon Toury has given himself the task of developing the descriptive branch of translation studies, in the firm belief that any theory of translation can only be elaborated on the basis of accurate and systematic descriptions of translational phenomena. Translation studies is for Toury an essentially empirical discipline, and as such it needs to look at how translations are produced and received, which implies that most of the attention on the part of researchers should go to the *target* pole of translation: 'translation are facts of the target culture' says one of Toury's (1995: 29) most famous formulations, and as such they need to be described with a proper contextualization in that culture. Toury's work on the application of norm theory to translation and his insistence on devising research methods appropriate for translation studies (and not borrowed wholesale from neighbouring disciplines such as linguistics) is to be seen in this light.

Toury's early theoretical work was conducted in the 1970s within the framework of **Polysystem Theory**, and mainly in relation to literary translation. The work he carried out in those years led to his 1980 book *In Search of a Theory of Translation*, which however only enjoyed limited circulation. It was in this book that Toury first delineated his theory of translational **norms**. In particular, he started from the assumption that translations occupy a position and fulfil a certain function in the social and literary systems of the target culture, and that this determines the particular strategies employed by translators. Such strategies, in turn, are based on the norms guiding the choices made by translators, seen as the notions of correctness or appropriateness that they adhere to in their work. Such notions are related to the receiving end of translation only, and it is in this sense that translations are to be seen primarily as facts of the target culture.

Toury's 1995 book *Descriptive Translation Studies and beyond* is an expansion and refinement of his earlier ideas, this time related to translation in general and not just to literary translation. The book delineates a fully fledged programme of descriptive research, seen as the necessary prerequisite for any treatment of translation at theoretical level. In particular, descriptions of translational phenomena should for Toury take into account as wide a variety as possible of conditions under which translation is carried out, at both individual and social level. The results of these descriptions must be brought to bear on the theoretical branch of the discipline but, as Toury (1995: 14–17) himself points out, the relationship between theory and description is 'bidirectional'. More specifically, Toury (1995: 15–16) sees translation studies as a discipline which aims at tackling three types of issues:

(1) all that translation *can* involve in principle;
(2) what translation *does* involve in principle;
(3) what translation *is likely* to involve under specified conditions.

Step (1) is basically theoretical and speculative; at this stage, hypotheses of an essentially logical nature can be made on, say, how metaphor is translated (cf. Toury 1995: 81–84). Step (2) carries out descriptive work, establishing the relevant variables and their impact on modes of translational behaviour; to continue with the example, it is at this stage that a corpus of texts is examined to see how metaphors are actually translated. Step (3) refines, at a theoretical level again, the initial hypotheses based on the descriptive work, and can either make predictions on future behaviour or put forward more elaborate hypotheses to be tested empirically; in the case of metaphors, based on the observation of actual translations in relation to certain TL contextual features, it may be hypothesized, for example, that their use in TTs is governed by a given target norm and has nothing to do with the nature of the source metaphors themselves.

The aim of translation studies is thus for Toury essentially of a *descriptive-explanatory* nature (as opposed, for instance, to the insistence on applied aims of other target-oriented approaches such as **skopos theory**). Within this framework, norms are a central notion as they are seen by Toury as capable of doing away with the need to define what translation 'is' in essential terms. Toury, in other words, proposes to look at what people take to be (good or bad) translations based on their own ideas of what (good or bad) translations should be like – and this, in turn, is taken by Toury as exerting a binding influence on how translators approach their task. The influence is binding because adherence to norms on the part of translators is sanctioned: negatively for those who violate them, positively for those who abide by them (Toury 1999: 16).

Norms thus provide the link between, on the one hand, the general values or ideas shared by a community as to what is right/wrong or adequate/inadequate and, on the other, the performance of translators observed in particular situations. They could be seen as the repertoire of habits, skills and styles based on which translators adopt certain strategies instead of others. In terms of the production of translations, they act as binding guidelines, as adherence to norms is sanctioned (positively or negatively, as we have seen). In terms of the **assessment** of translations, norms serve as parameters or yardsticks. Norms are *not* permanent laws: they are socio-cultural constraints affecting the **process of translation** as carried out by the translators who are active in a given culture, community or group. In particular, they have a 'graded and relative nature' (Toury 1999: 21) and are generally middle of the way between rules (objective norms) and idiosyncrasies (subjective norms).

More specifically, Toury (1995: 54–65) distinguishes two types of norms, both seen as historically, socially and culturally determined. *Preliminary norms* have to do with decisions of 'translation policy' (i.e. the choice of texts to be translated) and with the possibility to rely on 'indirect translation', or translation through an intermediate language. *Operational norms* govern the decisions taken during the act of translation as regards textual and linguistic aspects. Besides these two groups of norms, an *initial norm* is also assumed by Toury to govern the translator's 'basic choice between two polar alternatives' (1980: 54), the ST and the TL. When orienting the translation towards the ST, the translator is said to provide an *adequate* translation; when subscribing to the norms active in the TL, the translator is said to provide an *acceptable* translation. Thus, for example, a translation aiming at adequacy will essentially try to make sure that the basic rules of the TL system are not breached, while one aiming at acceptability will distance itself considerably from the formal and textual aspects of the original.

The particular norms that can be seen to have guided the translation of a text or group of texts can be reconstructed, for Toury, from two types of sources. One is the texts themselves, where 'regularities of behaviour' (1995: 55) can be observed and related to the contextual factors influencing the translation. The other source is represented by the explicit statements about translation norms made by translators, publishers, critics and the like; this second source, however, should be treated with circumspection, as explicit formulations of norms are likely to be biased and partial (Toury 1995: 65).

In the long run, as the descriptive analyses of translational phenomena cumulate findings, Toury considers it possible to arrive at the formulation of probabilistic laws of translation, which is however a task that lies 'beyond' the remit of descriptive studies. These laws are theoretical formulations which state the relations obtaining between a set of relevant variables. Being probabilistic, they are meant to state the likelihood that a particular behaviour (or linguistic realization) would occur under specified conditions, and are arrived at based on the findings provided by descriptive studies.

As an illustrative example, Toury (1995: 267–279) discusses two laws, the 'law of growing standardisation' and the 'law of interference'. The former says that 'in translation, source-text textmes tend to be converted into target-text repertoremes' (Toury 1995: 268) or, in other words, that the textual relations observed in the original texts (e.g. an unusual collocation) tend to be replaced by translators with relations that are more habitual in the target language (e.g. a fixed collocation). The law of interference says that ST linguistic features tend to be transferred to the TT, with the possibility of giving rise to negative transfer, i.e. deviations from codified TL practices. The two laws have appeared to run counter each other to some scholars (e.g. Chesterman 1997: 72), with interference pointing to the dominance of the SL and growing standardization pointing at the dominance of the TL. Pym (2008), however, shows that if the two laws are considered beyond the purely linguistic level, they can both be regarded as ways in which translators avoid the risk associated with given tasks: in other words, given the expectations of TL readers, in some cases translators may see a degree of interference as the safest option, whereas in other cases TL standardization will be seen as the most rewarding strategy.

Essential reading

Pym, A. (2008), 'On Toury's laws of how translators translate', in A. Pym, M. Shlesinger, M. and D. Simeoni (eds), *Beyond Descriptive Translation Studies*. Amsterdam/Philadelphia: Benjamins, pp. 311–328.

Toury, G. (1995), *Descriptive Translation Studies and Beyond*. Amsterdam/Philadelphia: Benjamins.

Toury, G. (1999), 'A handful of paragraphs on "translation" and "norms" ', in C. Schäffner (ed.), *Translation and Norms*. Clevedon: Multilingual Matters, pp. 9–31.

Lawrence Venuti

The work of Lawrence Venuti, an American translator and translation theorist, reflects and develops some of the major trends emerged in culturally oriented approaches to translation over the 1980s and 1990s. Showing particular affinity with hermeneutic and poststructuralist approaches to language and translation, Venuti has set himself the task of elaborating an ethically committed approach to translation, arguing for the adoption of forms of translating capable of providing increased visibility to the work of translators and thus aimed at overcoming the marginality of translation observed both in North-American academic circles and in the larger Anglo-American cultural scenario.

Operating in an area straddling cultural studies and translation studies, Venuti does not share the overemphasis on theory and speculation typical of the former yet at the same time criticizes the anti-intellectualism of the latter. In particular, he objects to the empiricism that, from his point of view, translation studies scholars often indulge in, which leads them to neglect such decisive aspects as the social and political contexts in which translators operate and translations are received: '[t]he empiricism that prevails in translation studies tends to privilege analytical concepts derived from linguistics, regardless of how narrow or limited they may be in their explanatory power' (Venuti 2003: 248). More specifically, Venuti sees empiricism as carrying two main limitations: (1) in devising complex analytical concepts, it provides too much detail to solve translation problems; and (2) it uses those concepts, which are essentially rooted in linguistics, as standards for the **assessment** of translations. In the long run, he claims, 'the empiricism in translation studies resists the sort of speculative thinking that encourages translators to reflect on the cultural, ethical, and political issues raised by their work' (2003: 249).

Venuti's own reflection (see particularly Venuti 1998, [1995] 2008) is on the situation and status of translation in the Anglo-American tradition. Venuti ([1995] 2008) provides an account of the history of translation from the 17th century onwards, showing how the canon of foreign literatures translated into English has been constructed mainly on the basis of one particular strategy, which he labels *domestication*. This strategy is concerned both with the mode of linguistic and stylistic transfer chosen for foreign texts and with the choice of texts to be translated. As a mode of translation, domestication entails translating in a transparent, fluent style, felt as capable of giving access to the ST author's precise meaning. This in turn influences the choice of texts to be translated, as these are selected largely for their capacity to be translated with a domesticating approach.

Venuti sees such a strategy aimed at producing fluent and transparent translations as having two main consequences. On the one hand, domesticated translation renders the work of translators ultimately invisible. Publishers, reviewers and readers expect a translated text to read like an original and therefore to present no linguistic or stylistic peculiarities. As translators strive to secure readability and adhere to current usage, readers are presented with the illusion of transparency and the translators' own work is made invisible. A second consequence of the domesticating approach has to do with the ethnocentric reduction of the foreign text to the values of the TL culture. Translation is for Venuti ([1995] 2008: 13f.) inevitably an act of 'violence': the multiplicity of potential meanings of a foreign text end up being fixed by any given translation, as translating is only possible 'on the strength of an interpretation' (13), especially for 'cultural forms open to interpretation such as literary texts, philosophical treatises, film subtitling, advertising copy, conference papers, and legal testimony' (19). In translation, the meaning of such texts is bound to be reconstituted according to TL values and beliefs and following 'hierarchies of dominance and marginality' (Venuti [1995] 2008: 14). Albeit inevitable, this reconstruction of meanings can nonetheless be directed towards different TL values and beliefs. Domesticating strategies in translation are ethnocentric in that they bring the *dominant* values and beliefs of the TL to bear on the foreign texts.

An alternative method to domestication, and one that Venuti sees as better equipped to register the irreducible differences obtaining in foreign texts, is *foreignization*, which Venuti conceptualizes in rather close adherence with the ideas of the French translator and translation theorist Antoine Berman ([1984] 1992). (Berman in turn, recovered the distinction between domesticating and foreignizing translation from the writings of the 19th-century German theologian and philosopher Friedrich Schleiermacher; see 'Introduction'.) Foreignization is a mode of translation which favours strategies that exploit resources available in the TL (e.g. its various registers, styles or dialects) to create a defamiliarizing yet intelligible effect in the translated text. For Venuti, foreignizing translation is not to be equated with literalness (as it tended to be in Berman), as he allows this general strategy of translation to take very different, even conflicting forms: not only close, resistant renderings, but also renderings that mix different cultural discourses, or even ones that are free and fluent. The two concepts of domestication and foreignization, in other words, must not be seen as acting exclusively on a linguistic or stylistic level. Rather, they are 'fundamentally ethical attitudes' (Venuti [1995] 2008: 19) towards a foreign text and culture, or two different ways of answering what Venuti sees as the central question of translation: given that translation always presupposes a 'domestic inscription' or a TL 'slant' (Venuti 2004) in the foreign text, what remedies can be sought in order to partially preserve or restore the foreignness so that it is not completely appropriated by the receiving culture? Venuti sees this as an essentially ethical question and he himself is very clear in declaring his preference for foreignizing, or 'resistant', forms translation. Although these can be as partial as domesticating translations, Venuti considers it ethically important that they are explicitly so. Illustrations of how forms of foreignizing translation can be enacted at the linguistic/stylistic level are presented as case studies scattered through most of Venuti's books and papers, often with reference to his own translating experience (see e.g. Venuti 1998, 2003).

Essential reading
Venuti, L. (1998), *The Scandals of Translation. Towards an Ethics of Difference*. London/New York: Routledge.

Venuti, L. (2003), 'Translating Derrida on translation: Relevance and disciplinary resistance', *The Yale Journal of Criticism*, 16(2), pp. 237–262.

Venuti, L. ([1995] 2008), *The Translator's Invisibility. A History of Translation*. London/New York: Routledge.

Hans J. Vermeer

The German scholar Hans J. Vermeer is one of the initiators of the radical change of paradigm that took place in the study of translation in the decade between 1975 and 1985, leading to a reassessment of the linguistically oriented approaches that had dominated the field in the previous decades. Kept firmly within the realm of applied linquistics, translation was till then looked at mainly in terms of a relationship of **equivalence** between ST and TT (e.g. as in Koller 1979) and its study was generally based on a 'scientific' approach rooted in linguistic theories, although already accepting insights from sociolinguistics (e.g. in Nida 1964) or communication theory (e.g. in Wilss 1982).

Following a lecture course on a 'General Theory of Translation' held in 1976–1977 (and attended by other scholars, such as Hans Hönig and Paul Kussmaul, who would later be associated with **functionalist approaches**), in 1978 Vermeer published an essay called 'Ein Rahmen für eine allgemeine Translationstheorie', where he lay the basis for what later came to be known as *Skopostheorie,* or **skopos theory**. This was further elaborated in subsequent works (e.g. Vermeer 1983) and then extensively presented in a book written by Vermeer together with Katharina Reiss: *Grundlegung einer allgemeinen Translationstheorie*, or 'Foundations for a General Theory of Translation' (Reiss and Vermeer 1984; for presentations of the theory written in English by Vermeer itself, see Vermeer 1989, 1996).

The book, divided in two parts, first presents a detailed illustration of *skopos* theory and then, in the second part, outlines a series of 'special' theories that adapt Reiss' **text typology** (which had been originally presented in Reiss 1971) to the more general model. The general theory is based on a view of translation as a form of *action*. As all action, it is governed by a certain aim or purpose, labelled *skopos* (Greek for 'purpose' or 'goal'). The *skopos* is thus the particular purpose for which a translator produces a new text in the TL (referred to as *translatum* by Vermeer). Merely **transcoding** an ST into the TL is not sufficient in order to produce an adequate translation; as the target text is produced in, and oriented towards, the target culture, the overriding factor in producing it is its particular *skopos* – which does not rule out that literal translation 'can be a legitimate translational skopos itself' (Vermeer 1989: 176).

In Vermeer and Reiss (1984: 134–136), five broad translation types are identified (the English translation of the label for each type is based on Snell-Hornby 2006: 52–53): an *interlinear version* is a text which reproduces the sequence of TL words disregarding TL rules; a *grammar translation* observes rules of usage in the TL but only serves illustrative purposes, e.g. in foreign language classes; a *documentary translation* is a text aimed at informing the reader of the ST content; a *communicative translation* is oriented towards the target culture and conforms to TL conventions; finally, an *adapting* translation is one where the ST is assimilated still further in the target culture in order to serve a particular function. Besides leading to the identification of these global strategies, the *skopos* concept can be used in relation to particular segments of a text (Vermeer 1989: 175), although Vermeer is not specific about how exactly the reproduction of ST segments at a micro-contextual level may be guided by the *skopos*.

In actual translation situations, the *skopos* of the translation is specified, implicitly or explicitly, by the client in the **translation brief** (see also Vermeer 1989: 182–187), and where the brief is not specific as to the ultimate purpose of the translation, this is usually apparent from the situation itself, so that, for instance, 'a technical article about some astronomical discovery is to be translated as technical article for astronomers [. . .]; or if a company wants a business letter translated, the natural assumption is that the letter will be used by the company' (1989: 183). Considering such assumptions valid, it can be concluded that any translation is carried out according to a *skopos* (1986: 183). To the critics who see *skopos* theory as unsuited for the description of literary translation, Vermeer (1989: 177–181) has responded that all texts, including literary works, have a purpose and that this may have been attached to them by readers or other users (e.g. publishers). The faithful imitation of the original found in many literary translations may be one legitimate *skopos* among others, possibly aimed at preserving the 'breadth of interpretation' of the ST.

In Vermeer's approach, traditional debates on what translation 'is' or what types of equivalence relationships it establishes with the ST become secondary, as they are seen to ignore the dynamism presupposed by the notion of *skopos* and inherent in any act of translation. Such dynamism implies that, even for the same text, different translations are possible, each prioritizing a particular function. Vermeer is always careful to stress that no particular goal or *skopos* is more appropriate than others in any translation situation, and that the ultimate aim of his theory is to make translators aware that *some* goal exits, that translation is never a purposeless activity and that a given text does not have one correct or best translation only (Vermeer 1983: 62–88).

Skopos theory takes into consideration the actual practice of translation and integrates it into its theoretical model to an extent that, at the time Vermeer's idea started to be circulated, might have appeared revolutionary for those still looking at translation in terms of static, contrastive descriptions of language. Vermeer's ideas, however, were developed in parallel to other theories and approaches which were focusing attention on the socio-cultural context in which translation takes place, thus contributing to what Vermeer himself has described as the 'dethroning' of the ST. **Gideon Toury**'s descriptive approach, for instance, was also bringing to the fore notions such as 'function' and 'culture', although considering them from different perspectives. **Juliane House**'s model of quality assessment, first presented in 1977, may be seen to share with skopos theory a holistic view of text, although House has always energetically rejected target-audience notions of translation appropriateness. The contemporary model which *skopos* theory shows the most affinity to is Holz-Mänttäri's (1984) theory of **translatorial action**, largely on account of the emphasis that both models place on the practice of translation. Over the years, Vermeer has included many of Holz-Mänttäri's ideas into his thinking, such as the view of the translator as an 'expert' or that of translation as the 'design' of a new text in the TL – a design which Vermeer sees as ultimately based on the *skopos* of the text.

Essential reading

Reiss, K. and Vermeer, H. J. (1984), *Grundlegung einer allgemeinen Translationstheorie*. Tübingen: Niemeyer.

Vermeer, H. J. (1989), 'Skopos and commission in translational action', in A. Chesterman (ed.), *Readings in Translation Theory*. Helsinki: Finn Lectura, pp. 173–187.

Vermeer, H. J. (1996), *A Skopos Theory of Translation (Some Arguments For and Against)*. Heidelberg: TEXTconTEXT.

Key Readings and Bibliography

Titles presented as key readings are preceded by the symbol '▶'. The section concludes with a list of the main journals and periodicals specializing in translation studies.

Aaltonen, S. (1997), 'Translating plays or baking apple pies: A functional approach to the study of drama translation', in M. Snell-Hornby, Z. Jettmarovà and K. Kaindl (eds), *Translation as Intercultural Communication. Selected Papers from the EST Congress – Prague 1995*. Amsterdam/Philadelphia: Benjamins, pp. 89–97.

Adab, B. (2005), 'Translating into a second language: Can we, should we?', in G. Anderman and M. Rogers (eds), *In and Out of English: For Better, For Worse?* Clevedon: Multilingual Matters, pp. 227–241.

Alves, F. (ed.) (2003), *Triangulating Translation. Perspectives in Process Oriented Research*. Amsterdam/Philadelphia: Benjamins.

Anderman, G. (2005), *Europe on Stage. Translation and Theatre*. London: Oberon.

Appiah, K. A. (1993), 'Thick Translation'. *Callaloo*, 16(4), 808–819. Reprinted in Venuti (2004), pp. 389–401.

Baker, M. (1992), *In Other Words. A Coursebook on Translation*. London/New York: Routledge.

▶ Baker, M. (1995), 'Corpora in Translation Studies: An overview and some suggestions for future research', *Target*, 7(2), pp. 223–243.

Baker, M. (1996), 'Corpus-based Translation Studies: The challenges that lie ahead', in H. Somers (ed.), *Terminology, LSP and Translation. Studies in Language Engineering in Honour of Juan C. Sager*. Amsterdam/Philadelphia: Benjamins, pp. 175–186.

▶ Baker, M. (ed.) (1998), *Routledge Encyclopedia of Translation Studies*. London/New York: Routledge.

Baker, M. (2006), *Translation and Conflict: A Narrative Account*. London/ New York: Routledge.

Ballard, M. (1992), *De Cicéron à Benjamin: Traducteurs, traductions, réflexions*. Lille: Presses Universitaires de Lille.

Barkhudarov, L. (1993), 'The problem of the unit of translation', in P. Zlateva (ed.), *Translation as Social Action*. London/New York: Routledge, pp. 39–46.

▶ Bassnett, S. ([1980] 2002), *Translation Studies*. London/New York: Routledge.

▶ Bassnett, S. and Lefevere, A. (eds) (1990), *Translation, History and Culture*. London: Pinter.

Bassnett, S. and Trivedi, H. (eds) (1999), *Post-colonial Translation. Theory and Practice*. London/New York: Routledge.

Bastin, G. (1998), 'Adaptation', in M. Baker (ed.), *Routledge Encyclopedia of Translation Studies*. London/New York: Routledge, pp. 5–8.

Bell, R. (1991), *Translation and Translating. Theory and Practice*. London: Longman.

Benjamin, W. ([1923] 1963), 'Die Aufgabe des Übersetzers', in H. J. Störig (ed.), *Das Problem des Übersetzens*. Darmstadt: Wissenschaftliche Buchgesellschaft, pp. 182–195.

▶ Berman, A. (1984), *L'épreuve de l'étranger. Culture et traduction dans l'Allemagne romantique*. Paris: Gallimard (*The Experience of the Foreign. Culture and Translation in Romantic Germany*. Translated by S. Heyvaert. Albany: SUNY, 1992).

Bernardini, S. (2001), 'Think-Aloud Protocols in translation research: Achievements, limits, future prospects', *Target*, 13(2), pp. 241–263.

▶ Blum Kulka, S. (1986), 'Shifts of coherence and cohesion in translation', in J. House and S. Blum Kulka (eds), *Interlingual and Intercultural Communication. Discourse and Cognition in Translation and Second Language Acquisition Studies*. Tübingen: Narr, pp. 17–35. Reprinted in Venuti (2004), pp. 298–313.

Cabré, M. T. (2003), *Terminology. Theory, Methods and Applications*. Amsterdam/Philadelphia: Benjamins.

▶ Campbell, S. (1998), *Translation into the Second Language*. Harlow: Longman.

▶ Catford, J. C. (1965), *A Linguistic Theory of Translation*. London: Oxford University Press.

Chamberlain, L. (1988), 'Gender and the metaphorics of translation', *Signs*, 13, pp. 454–472. Reprinted in L. Venuti (ed.) (2004), pp. 306–321.

▶ Chesterman, A. (1993), 'From "is" to "ought": Laws, norms and strategies in Translation Studies', *Target*, 5(1), pp. 1–20.

▶ Chesterman, A. (1997), *Memes of Translation. The Spread of Ideas in Translation Theory*. Amsterdam/Philadelphia: Benjamins.

Chesterman, A. (1998), *Contrastive Functional Analysis*. Amsterdam/Philadelphia: Benjamins.

Chesterman, A. (2000a), 'A causal model for Translation Studies', in M. Olohan (ed.), *Intercultural Faultlines. Research Models in Translation Studies I. Textual and Cognitive Aspects*. Manchester: St Jerome, pp. 15–27.

Chesterman, A. (2000b), 'Memetics and translation strategies', *Synapse*, 5, pp. 1–17.

Chesterman, A. (2001), 'Proposal for a Hieronymic Oath', *The Translator*, 7(2), pp. 139–154.

Chesterman, A. (2004a), 'Translation as an object of reflection and scholarly discourse', in H. Kittel, A. P. Frank, N. Greiner, T. Hermans, W. Koller, J. Lambert and F. Paul (eds), *Übersetzung / Translation / Traduction*. Berlin: Mouton de Gruyter, pp. 93–100.

Chesterman, A. (2004b), 'Hypotheses about translation universals', in G. Hansen, K. Malmkjær and D. Gile (eds), *Claims, Changes and Challenges in Translation Studies*. Amsterdam/Philadelphia: Benjamins, pp. 1–13.

Chesterman, A. and Arrojo, R. (2000), 'Forum: Shared Ground in Translation Studies', *Target*, 12(1), pp. 151–160.

▶ Chesterman, A. and Wagner, E. (2002), *Can Theory Help Translators? A Dialogue Between the Ivory Tower and the Wordface*. Manchester: St Jerome.

Cronin, M. (1996), *Translating Ireland: Translation, Languages, Cultures*. Cork: Cork University Press.

Cronin, M. (2003), *Translation and Globalization*. London/New York: Routledge.

Delisle, J. (1988), *Translation: An Interpretive Approach*. Ottawa: University of Ottawa Press.

▶ Delisle, J., Lee-Janke, H. and Cormier, M. C. (eds) (1999), *Terminologie de la traduction / Translation Terminology / Terminologia de la traducción / Terminologie der Übersetzung*. Amsterdam/Philadelphia: Benjamins.

▶ Delisle, J., Woodsworth, J. (eds) (1995), *Translators through History*. Amsterdam/Philadelphia: Benjamins/Unesco.

Díaz Cintas, J. (2005), 'El subtitulado y los avances tecnológicos', in R. Merino, J. M. Santamaría and E. Pajares (eds), *Trasvases culturales: Literatura, Cine y traducción 4*. Vitoria: Universidad del País Vasco, pp. 155–175.

Díaz Cintas, J. and Remael, A. (2007), *Audiovisual Translation: Subtitling*. Manchester: St Jerome.

Esselink, B. (2003), 'Localization and translation', in H. Somers (ed.), *Computers and Translation*. Amsterdam/Philadelphia: Benjamins, pp. 67–86.

▶ Even-Zohar, I. (1978), 'The position of translated literature within the literary polysystem', in J. S. Holmes, J. Lambert and R. van den Broeck (eds), *Literature and Translation: New Perspectives in Literary Studies*. Leuven: Acco, pp. 117–127.

Fawcett, P. (1995), 'Translation and power play', *The Translator*, 1(2), pp. 177–192.

Fawcett, P. (2000), 'Translation in the Broadsheets', *The Translator*, 6(2), pp. 295–307.

von Flotow, L. (1997), *Translation and Gender: Translating in the 'Era of Feminism'*. Manchester: St Jerome.

von Flotow, L. (ed.) (2000a), *Idéologie et traduction / Ideology and Translation*. Numéro special de *TTR*, 13(1).

von Flotow, L. (2000b), 'Women, Bibles, Ideologies', *TTR*, 13(1), pp. 9–20.

Fraser, J. (1996), 'The translator investigated. Learning from translation process analysis', *The Translator*, 2(1), pp. 65–79.

Frawley, W. (1984), 'Prolegomenon to a theory of translation', in W. Frawley (ed.), *Translation: Literary, Linguistic, and Philosoph-*

ical Perspectives. London/Toronto: Associated University Press, pp. 159–175.

▶ Gambier, Y. (ed.) (2004), *Audiovisual Translation.* Numéro special de *Meta*, 49(1).

▶ Gambier, Y. and Gottlieb, H. (eds), (2001), *(Multi) Media Translation.* Amsterdam/Philadelphia: Benjamins.

▶ Gile, D. (1995), *Basic Concepts and Models for Interpreter and Translator Training.* Amsterdam/Philadelphia: Benjamins.

Gouadec, D. (1989), 'Comprendre, évaluer, prévenir. Pratique, enseignement et recherche face à l'erreur et à la faute en traduction', *TTR*, 2(2), pp. 35–54.

Gouadec, D. (1990), 'Traduction signalétique', *Meta*, 35(2), pp. 332–341.

▶ Gouadec, D. (2007), *Translation as a Profession.* Amsterdam/ Philadelphia: Benjamins.

Gouanvic, J.-M. (1997), 'Translator and the shape of things to come: The emergence of American science fiction in post-war France', *The Translator*, 3(2), pp. 125–152.

▶ Gutt, E.-A. ([1991] 2000), *Translation and Relevance: Cognition and Context.* Manchester: St Jerome [1st ed. published by Blackwell].

Hale, S. and Campbell, S. (2002), 'The interaction between text difficulty and translation accuracy', *Babel*, 48(1), pp. 14–33.

Halliday, M. A. K. and Hasan, R. (1976), *Cohesion in English.* London: Longman.

Halverson, S. (1997), 'The concept of equivalence in translation: Much ado about something', *Target*, 9(2), pp. 207–233.

Halverson, S. (1999), 'Conceptual work and the "translation" concept', *Target*, 9(2), pp. 1–31.

Harris, B. (1977), 'The importance of natural translation', *Working Papers on Bilingualism*, 12, pp. 96–114.

Harvey, K. (1995), 'A descriptive framework for compensation', *The Translator*, 1(1), 65–86.

Harvey, K. (2000), 'Gay community, gay identity and the translated text', *TTR*, 13(1), 137–165.

Hatim, B. (2001), *Teaching and Researching Translation*. Harlow: Longman.

▶ Hatim, B. and Mason, I. (1990), *Discourse and the Translator*. London/New York: Longman.

▶ Hatim, B. and Mason, I. (1997), *The Translator as Communicator*. London/New York: Routledge.

▶ Hermans, T. (ed.) (1985), *The Manipulation of Literature Studies in Literary Translation*. London: Croom Helm.

Hermans, T. (1999), *Translation in Systems. Descriptive and System-oriented Approaches Explained*. Manchester: St Jerome.

Hickey, L. (1998), *The Pragmatics of Translation*. Clevedon: Multilingual Matters.

Hönig, H. and Kussmaul, P. (1982), *Strategie der Übersetzung: Ein Lehr- und Arbeitsbuch*. Tübingen: Narr.

▶ Holmes, J. S. (1988), *Translated! Papers on Literary Translation and Translation Studies*. Amsterdam: Rodopi.

▶ Holz-Mänttäri, J. (1984), *Translatorisches Handeln: Theorie und Methode*. Helsinki: Suomalainen Tiedeakatemia.

▶ House, J. (1977), *A Model for Translation Quality Assessment*. Tübingen: Narr.

▶ House, J. (1997), *Translation Quality Assessment. A Model Revisited*. Tübingen: Narr.

House, J. (1998), 'Politeness and translation', in L. Hickey (ed.), *The Pragmatics of Translation*. Clevedon: Multilingual Matters, pp. 54–72.

Hutchins, W. J. and Somers, H. L. (1992), *An Introduction to Machine Translation*. London/San Diego: Academic Press.

Inghilleri, M. (ed.) (2005), *Bourdieu and the Sociology of Translation and Interpreting*. Special Issue of *The Translator*, 11(2).

Jääskeläinen, R. (1993), 'Investigating translation strategies', in S. Tirkkonen-Condit, (ed.), *Recent Trends in Empirical Translation Research*. Joensuu: University of Joensuu Faculty of Arts, pp. 99–120.

Jääskeläinen, R. and Tirkkonen-Condit, S. (1991), 'Automatised processes in professional vs. non-professional translation: A think-aloud protocol study', in S. Tirkkonen-Condit (ed.), *Empirical Research in Translation and Intercultural Studies*. Tübingen: Narr, pp. 89–109.

Jacquemond, R. (1992), 'Translation and cultural hegemony: The case of French-Arabic translation', in L. Venuti (ed.), *Rethinking Translation. Discourse, Subjectivity, Ideology*. London/New York: Routledge, pp. 139–158.

Jakobsen, A. L. (1999), 'Logging target text production with *Translog*', in G. Hansen (ed.), *Probing the Process in Translation. Methods and Results*. Copenhagen Studies in Language 24. Copenhagen: Samfundslitteratur, pp. 9–20.

▶ Jakobson, R. (1959), 'On linguistic aspects of translation', in R. A. Brower (ed.), *On Translation*. Cambridge, Mass.: Harvard University Press, pp. 232–239. Reprinted in Venuti (2004), pp. 138–143.

Jakobson, R. (1960), 'Closing statement: Linguistics and poetics', in T. A. Sebeok (ed.), *Style in Language*. Cambridge, MA: MIT Press, pp. 350–377.

James, C. (1989), 'Genre analysis and the translator', *Target*, 1(1), pp. 29–41.

Katan, D. (2004), *Translating Cultures. An Introduction for Translators, Interpreters and Mediators*. Manchester: St Jerome.

▶ Kenny, D. (2001), *Lexis and Creativity in Translation. A Corpus-based Study*. Manchester: St Jerome.

Kiraly, D. (2000), *A Social Constructivist Approach to Translator Education*. Manchester: St Jerome.

▶ Krings, H. P. (1986), *Was in den Köpfen von Übersetzern vorgeht. Eine empirische Untersuchung der Struktur des Übersetzungsprozesses an fortgeschrittenen Französischlernern*. Tübingen: Narr.

▶ Koller, W. (1979), *Einführung in die Übersetzungswissenschaft*. Heidelberg: Quelle & Meyer.

Kuhiwczak, P. and Littau, K. (eds) (2007), *A Companion to Translation Studies*. Clevedon: Multilingual Matters.

▶ Kussmaul, P. (1995), *Training the Translator*. Amsterdam/Philadelphia: Benjamins.

▶ Lambert, J. (1989), 'La traduction, les langues et la communication de masse. Les ambiguïtés du discours international', *Target*, 1(2), pp. 215–237.

▶ Laviosa, S. (2002), *Corpus-based Translation Studies: Theory, Findings, Applications*. Amsterdam: Rodopi.

▶ Lefevere, A. (1992), *Translation, Rewriting, and the Manipulation of Literary Fame*. London/New York: Routledge.

Lefevere, A. (1998), 'Translation practice(s) and the circulation of cultural capital. Some Aeneids in English', in S. Bassnett and A. Lefevere, *Constructing Cultures: Essays on Literary Translation*. Clevedon: Multilingual Matters, pp. 41–56.

van Leuven-Zwart, K. M. (1989/1990), 'Translation and original: Similarities and dissimilarities', I and II, *Target*, 1(2), pp. 151–181, and 2(1), pp. 69–95.

▶ Levý, J. (1967), 'Translation as a decision process', in *To Honor Roman Jakobson*. The Hague: Mouton, vol. 2, pp. 1171–1182. Reprinted in Chesterman (1989), pp. 37–52.

Lewis, P. E. (1985), 'The measures of translation effects', in J. Graham (ed.), *Difference in Translation*. Ithaca, NY: Cornell University Press, pp. 31–62.

Livbjerg, I. and Mees, I. M. (2003), 'Patterns of dictionary use in non-domain-specific translation', in F. Alves (ed.), *Triangulating Translation. Perspectives in Process Oriented Research*. Amsterdam/Philadelphia: Benjamins, pp. 123–136.

Lörscher, W. (1991), *Translation Performance, Translation Process and Translation Strategies. A Psycholinguistic Investigation*. Tübingen: Narr.

Mauranen, A. (2007), 'Universal tendencies in translation', in G. Anderman and M. Rogers (eds), *Incorporating Corpora. The Linguist and the Translator*. Clevedon: Multilingual Matters, pp. 32–48.

▶ Mauranen, A. and Kujamäki, P. (eds) (2004), *Translation Universals – Do They Exist?* Amsterdam/Philadelphia: Benjamins.

McEnery, T. and Xiao, Z. (2007), 'Parallel and comparable corpora: What is happening?', in M. Rogers and G. Anderman (eds), *Incorporating Corpora. The Linguist and the Translator*. Clevedon: Multilingual Matters, pp. 18–31.

Mossop, B. (2001), *Revising and Editing for Translators*. Manchester: St Jerome.

▶ Mossop, B. (2006), 'From culture to business. Federal government translation in Canada', *The Translator*, 12(1), pp. 1–27.

Munday, J. (2001), *Introducing Translation Studies. Theories and Applications*. London/New York: Routledge.

Munday, J. and Cunico, S. (eds) (2007), *Translation and Ideology. Encounters and Clashes*. Special Issue of *The Translator*, 13(2).

Neubert, A. (1985), *Translation and Text*. Leipzig: Enzyklopädie.

▶ Newmark, P. (1981), *Approaches to Translation*. Oxford: Pergamon.

▶ Newmark, P. (1988), *A Textbook of Translation*. New York/London: Prentice Hall.

▶ Nida, E. A. (1964), *Toward a Science of Translating: With Special Reference to Principles and Procedures Involved in Bible Translating*. Leiden: E. J. Brill.

Nida, E. A. ([1969] 1989), 'Science of translation', in A. Chesterman (ed.), *Readings in Translation Theory*. Helsinki: Finn Lectura, pp. 80–98. Originally published in: *Language*, 45(3), 1969, pp. 483–498.

Nida, E. A. and Taber, C. R. (1969), *The Theory and Practice of Translation*. Leiden: E. J. Brill.

▶ Niranjana, T. (1992), *Siting Translation: History Post-structuralism, and the Colonial Context*. Berkeley/Los Angeles: University of California Press.

Nord, C. (1991), *Text Analysis in Translation. Theory, Methodology and Didactic Application of a Model of Translation-oriented Text Analysis*. Amsterdam: Rodopi.

▶ Nord, C. (1997), *Translating as a Purposeful Activity. Functionalist Approaches Explained*. Manchester: St Jerome.

Olohan, M. (2004), *Introducing Corpora in Translation Studies*. London/New York: Routledge.

Orero, P. (ed.) (2004), *Topics in Audiovisual Translation*. Amsterdam/Philadelphia: Benjamins.

PACTE (2005), 'Investigating translation competence: Conceptual and methodological issues', *Meta*, 50(2), pp. 609–619.

Pokorn, N. (2005), *Challenging the Traditional Axioms: Translation into a Non-mother Tongue*. Amsterdam/Philadelphia: Benjamins.

Pym A. (1992), 'Translation error analysis and the interface with language teaching', in C. Dollerup and A. Loddegaard (eds), *Teaching Translation and Interpreting*. Amsterdam/Philadelphia: John Benjamins, pp. 279–288.

▶ Pym, A. (1995), 'European translation studies, *une science qui dérange*, and why equivalence needn't be a dirty word', *TTR*, 8(1), pp. 153–176.

▶ Pym, A. (1998), *Method in Translation History*. Manchester: St Jerome.

Pym, A. (2000), 'On cooperation', in M. Olohan (ed.), *Intercultural Faultlines. Research Models in Translation Studies I. Textual and Cognitive Aspects*. Manchester: St Jerome, pp. 181–192.

Pym, A. (2003), 'Redefining translation competence in an electronic age. In defence of a minimalist approach', *Meta*, 48(4), pp. 481–497.

Pym A. (2004), 'Text and risk in translation', in M. Sidiropoulou and A. Papaconstantinou (eds), *Choice and Difference in Translation. The Specifics of Transfer*. Athens: University of Athens, pp. 27–42.

Pym, A. (2006), 'Globalization and the politics of translation studies', *Meta*, 51(4), pp. 744–757.

Pym, A. (2008), 'On Toury's laws of how translators translate', in A. Pym, M. Shlesinger, M. and D. Simeoni (eds), *Beyond Descriptive Translation Studies*. Amsterdam/Philadelphia: Benjamins, pp. 311–328.

Quah, C. K. (2006), *Translation and Technology*. Basingstoke/New York: Palgrave Macmillan.

Quine, W. V. O. (1959), 'Translation and meaning', in R. A. Brower (ed.), *On Translation*, Cambridge, MA.: Harvard University Press, pp. 232–239.

Quine, W. V. O. (1960), *Word and Object*. Cambridge, MA.: MIT Press.

Rafael, L. V. (1993), *Contracting Colonialism: Translation and Christian Conversion in Tagalog Society under Early Spanish Rule*. Durham, NC: Duke University Press.

▶ Reiss, K. (1971), *Möglichkeiten und Grenzen der Übersetzungskritik*. München: Max Hueber (*Translation Criticism: The Potentials and Limitations*. Translated by E. F. Rhodes. Manchester: St Jerome, 2000).

▶ Reiss, K. and Vermeer, H. J. (1984), *Grundlegung einer allgemeinen Translationstheorie*. Tübingen: Niemeyer.

▶ Robinson, D. (1991), *The Translator's Turn*. Baltimore, MD: Johns Hopkins University Press.

Robinson, D. (1997a), *Translation and Empire. Postcolonial Approaches Explained*. Manchester: St Jerome.

Robinson, D. (ed.) (1997b), *Western Translation Theory from Herodotus to Nietzsche*. Manchester: St Jerome.

Robinson, D. (1998), 'Free translation', in M. Baker (ed.), *Routledge Encyclopedia of Translation Studies*. London/New York: Routledge, pp. 87–90.

▶ Robinson, D. ([1997] 2003), *Becoming a Translator. An Introduction to the Theory and Practice of Translation*. London/New York: Routledge.

Rogers, M. (2006), 'Structuring information in English: A specialist translation perspective on sentence beginnings', *The Translator*, 12(1), 29–64.

Rundle, C. (2000), 'The censorship of translation in Fascist Italy', *The Translator*, 6(1), pp. 67–86.

Sager, J. C. (1983), 'Quality and standards – The evaluation of translations', in C. Picken (ed.), *The Translator's Handbook*. London: Aslib, pp. 121–128.

▶ Sager, J. C. (1994), *Language Engineering and Translation. Consequences of Automation*. Amsterdam/Philadelphia: Benjamins.

Scarpa, F. (2008), *La traduzione specializzata. Un approccio didattico e professionale*, 2ª edizione. Milano: Hoepli.

Schäffner, C. (ed.) (1998), *Translation and Quality*. Clevedon: Multilingual Matters.

▶ Schäffner, C. (ed.) (1999), *Translation and Norms*. Clevedon: Multilingual Matters.

Schäffner, C. (2007), 'Politics and translation', in P. Kuhiwczak and K. Littau (eds), *A Companion to Translation Studies*. Clevedon: Multilingual Matters, pp. 134–147.

Schäffner, C. and Adab, B. (1997), 'Translation as intercultural communication – Contact as conflict', in M. Snell-Hornby, Z. Jettmarovà and K. Kaindl (eds), *Translation as Intercultural Communication. Selected Papers from the EST Congress – Prague 1995*. Amsterdam/ Philadelphia: Benjamins, pp. 325–327.

Schäffner, C. and Adab, B. (eds) (2000), *Developing Translation Competence*. Amsterdam/Philadelphia: Benjamins.

Seleskovitch, D. (1976), 'Interpretation. A psychological approach to translating', in R. W. Brislin (ed.), *Translation: Applications and Research*. New York: Gardner Press, pp. 92–116.

▶ Shuttleworth, M. and Cowie, M. (1997), *Dictionary of Translation Studies*. Manchester: St Jerome.

▶ Simeoni, D. (1998), 'The pivotal status of the translator's habitus', *Target*, 10(1), 1–39.

▶ Simon, S. (1996), *Gender in Translation. Cultural identities and the politics of transmission*. London/New York: Routledge.

▶ Snell-Hornby, M. (1988), *Translation Studies. An Integrated Approach*. Amsterdam/Philadelphia: Benjamins.

Snell-Hornby, M. (1996), ' "All the world's a stage": Multimedia translation – Constraint or potential', in C. Heiss and R. Bollettieri Bosinelli (eds), *Traduzione multimediale per il cinema, la televisione e la scena*. Forlì: CLUEB, pp. 29–45.

Snell-Hornby, M. (2001), 'The space "in between": What is a hybrid text?', *Across Languages and Cultures*, 2(2), pp. 207–216.

▶ Snell-Hornby, M. (2006), *The Turns of Translation Studies*. Amsterdam/Philadelphia: Benjamins.

Snell-Hornby, M. (2007), 'Theatre and opera translation', in P. Kuhiwczak and K. Littau (eds), *A Companion to Translation Studies*. Clevedon: Multilingual Matters, pp. 106–119.

Sorvali, I. (2004), 'The problem of the unit of translation: A linguistic perspective', in H. Kittel, A. P. Frank, N. Greiner, T. Hermans, W. Koller, J. Lambert and F. Paul (eds), *Übersetzung / Translation / Traduction*. Berlin: Mouton de Gruyter, pp. 354–362.

▶ Steiner, G. (1975), *After Babel*. Oxford: Oxford University Press.

Sturge, K. (2004), *'The Alien Within': Translation into German during the Nazi Regime*. Munich: Iudicium.

Taylor, C. (2004), 'Multimodal text analysis and subtitling', in E. Ventola, C. Cassily and M. Kaltenbacher (eds), *Perspectives on Multimodality*. Amsterdam/Philadelphia: Benjamins, pp. 153–172.

Tirkkonen-Condit, S. (2004), 'Unique items – Over- or under-represented in translated language', in A. Mauranen and P. Kujamäki (eds), *Translation Universals – Do They Exist?*. Amsterdam/Philadelphia: Benjamins, pp. 177–184.

Tirkkonen-Condit, S. and Jääskeläinen, R. (eds) (2000), *Tapping and Mapping the Processes of Translating and Interpreting. Outlooks on Empirical Research*. Amsterdam/Philadelphia: Benjamins.

▶ Toury, G. (1980), *In Search of a Theory of Translation*. Tel Aviv: The Porter Institute for Poetics and Semiotics, Tel Aviv University.

Toury, G. (1982), 'A rationale for descriptive translation studies', *Dispositio*, 7, pp. 23–29.

▶ Toury, G. (1995), *Descriptive Translation Studies and Beyond*. Amsterdam/Philadelphia: Benjamins.

Toury, G. (1999), 'A handful of paragraphs on "translation" and "norms"', in C. Schäffner (ed.), *Translation and Norms*. Clevedon: Multilingual Matters, pp. 9–31.

Toury, G. (2002), 'What's the problem with "Translation Problem"'?, in B. Lewandowska-Tomaszczyk, B. and M. Thelen (eds), *Translation and Meaning Part 6*. Maastricht: Hogeschool Zuyd, Maastricht School of Translation and Interpretation, pp. 57–71.

▶ Trosborg, A. (ed.) (1997), *Text Typology and Translation*. Amsterdam/Philadelphia: Benjamins.

Tymoczko, M. (1990), 'Translation in oral tradition as a touchstone for translation theory and practice', in S. Bassnett and A. Lefevere (eds), *Translation, History and Culture*. London: Pinter, pp. 46–55.

Tymoczko, M. (1999a), *Translation in a Postcolonial Context: Early Irish Literature in English Translation*. Manchester: St Jerome.

Tymoczko, M. (1999b), 'Post-colonial writing and literary translation', in S. Bassnett and H. Trivedi (eds), *Postcolonial Translation. Theory and Practice*. London/New York: Routledge, pp. 19–40.

Tymoczko, M. (2005), 'Trajectories of research in translation studies', *Meta*, 50(4), 1082–1097.

▶ Tymoczko, M. (2007), *Enlarging Translation, Empowering Translators*. Manchester: St Jerome.

Ulrych, M. (1999), *Focus on the Translator in a Multidisciplinary Perspective*. Padova: Unipress.

▶ Venuti, L. (ed.) (1992), *Rethinking Translation. Discourse, Subjectivity, Ideology*. London/New York: Routledge.

Venuti, L. (1998), *The Scandals of Translation. Towards an Ethics of Difference*. London/New York: Routledge.

Venuti, L. (2003), 'Translating Derrida on translation: Relevance and disciplinary resistance', *The Yale Journal of Criticism*, 16(2), pp. 237–262.

▶ Venuti, L. (ed.) (2004), *The Translation Studies Reader*. London/New York: Routledge.

Venuti, L. (2007), 'Translation Studies', in D. G. Nicholls (ed.), *Introduction to Scholarship in Modern Languages and Literatures*. New York: The Modern Language Association of America, pp. 294–311.

▶ Venuti, L. ([1995] 2008), *The Translator's Invisibility. A History of Translation*. London/New York: Routledge.

Vermeer, H. J. (1983), *Aufsätze zur Translationstheorie*. Heidelberg: Mimeo.

Vermeer, H. J. (1986), 'Übersetzen als kultureller Transfer', in M. Snell-Hornby (ed.), *Übersetzungswissenschaft–EineNeuorientierung*. Tübingen: Francke, pp. 30–53.

Vermeer, H. J. (1989), 'Skopos and commission in translational action', in A. Chesterman (ed.), *Readings in Translation Theory*. Helsinki: Finn Lectura, pp. 173–187.

Vermeer, H. J. (1992), *Skizzen zu einer Geschichte der Translation*. Vols 1 and 2. Frankfurt am Main: Verlag für Interkulturelle Kommunikation.

▶ Vermeer, H. J. (1996), *A Skopos Theory of Translation (Some Arguments For and Against)*. Heidelberg: TEXTconTEXT.

Vermeer, H. J. (1997), 'Translation and the "Meme" ', *Target*, 9(1), pp. 155–166.

Vieira, E. (1999), 'Liberating Calibans: Readings of Antropofagia and Haroldo de Campos' poetics of transcreation', in S. Bassnett and H. Trivedi (eds), *Post-colonial Translation. Theory and Practice*. London/New York: Routledge, pp. 95–113.

▶ Vinay, J.-P. and Darbelnet, J. ([1958] 1995), *Comparative Stylistics of French and English : A Methodology*. Translated and edited by J. Sager and M.-J. Hamel. Amsterdam/Philadelphia: Benjamins. Originally published as: *Stylistique comparée du français et de l'anglais. Méthode de traduction*. Paris: Didier, 1958.

Waddington, C. (1999), *Estudio comparativo de diferentes métodos de evaluación de traducción general (Inglés-Español)*. Madrid: Universidad Pontificia Comillas.

Wilss, W. (1982), *The Science of Translation. Problems and Methods*. Tübingen: Narr.

Wolf, M. (2002), 'Translation activity between culture, society and the individual: Towards a sociology of translation', in K. Harvey (ed.), *CTIS Occasional Papers* 2. Manchester: UMIST, pp. 33–43.

Journals and periodicals specializing in translation studies

Across Languages and Cultures: A Multidisciplinary Journal for Translation and Interpreting Studies

Babel: Revue internationale de la traduction / International Journal of Translation

JoSTrans – The Journal of Specialised Translation (an online journal available at: http://www.jostrans.org/)

Meta: Journal des traducteurs / Translator's Journal

New Voices in Translation Studies (an online journal available at: http://www.iatis.org/newvoices/)

Perspectives: Studies in Translatology

Target: International Journal on Translation Studies

The Interpreter and Translator Trainer (ITT)

The Translator: Studies in Intercultural Communication

Translation Studies

TTR: Traduction, Terminologie, Rédaction

Translation Studies Abstracts

Translation Studies Bibliography

Index